DUE DATE

			Printed in USA

D1115798

SATELLITE SURVEILLANCE

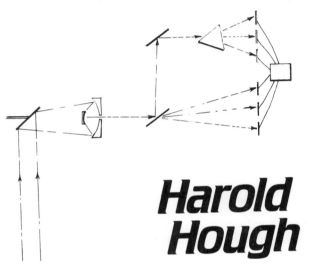

Harold Hough

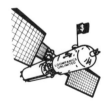

Loompanics Unlimited
Port Townsend, Washington

Other books by Harold Hough available from Loompanics Unlimited:

- *A Practical Guide to Photographic Intelligence*
- *Freedom Road*

This book is sold for informational purposes only. Neither the author nor the publisher will be held accountable for the use or misuse of the information contained in this book.

Published by:
Loompanics Unlimited
PO Box 1197
Port Townsend, WA 98368
Loompanics Unlimited is a division of Loompanics Enterprises, Inc.

ISBN 1-55950-077-8
Library of Congress Catalog Card Number 91-076488

G
70.4
.H81
1991

Contents

Dedication
To Helene

*She and the other spouses of military attaches
were counting tanks and avoiding Soviets
long before spy satellites. They were
the best intelligence bargain the
US ever had.*

Acknowledgements

I want to thank all the people who helped me while I was writing this book. Most of all, I want to thank Sandra Perry. Her infectious enthusiasm for satellite imagery and her clear explanations made the technology understandable. Without her help, this book would have been impossible.

Others also helped me along the way. People like Jennifer Visick, Dr. John P. Ford, Nicola McAlister Noll, Kevin Corbley, Dr. Velon Minshew, Don Hemenway, Pat McGarrity, Pat Harrison, Camal Dharamdial, Lyle Slater, and Tom Swaton all came through when I needed help.

I also want to thank the following groups: Autometrics, Barrainger Laboratories, The Orthoshop, Photometrics, and the American Society for Photogrammetry and Remote Sensing for their help in providing information.

A special thanks goes to the companies who provided the photographs in this book: EOSAT, The Jet Propulsion Laboratories, Central Trading Systems, The Orthoshop, The Pima Air Museum, and Autometric.

Finally, thanks goes to my wife, Ellen, who had to tolerate my babbling about satellites for what must have seemed like an eternity. And, of course, Clifford, my cat, who proofread my manuscript while sitting on my shoulder.

Introduction

A constellation of satellites circles the earth, photographing everyone and everything. The photographs may end up on the desk of someone in the CIA or KGB, in the dirty hands of a geologist in Equatorial Africa, or on the monitor of a political aide planning for the next election.

Satellites aren't just the stuff of spy novels. Every day satellite photographs are used by people who wouldn't know the CIA from a CPA. They're the product of a growing industry that helps us find oil, build expressways, cut lumber, and report the news. In fact, you can buy satellite photographs for the cost of a night on the town.

Despite its availability, few people know about space photography or appreciate its applications. Most can remember seeing pictures in magazines, but they don't realize the need for satellite photographs as a major force behind our space effort. Nor do they realize that space photographs are responsible for our ability to monitor strategic arms agreements and to find new mineral deposits.

What the public doesn't know about satellite imagery, those who use it aren't about to tell them. Many of the analysts are part of the intelligence community and are sworn to secrecy. The rest are scientists, who often make satellite imagery seem too complicated.

As a result, a big hole exists in satellite literature between the "gee whiz" articles in magazines and the technical books written for the industry. This hasn't benefited the satellite industry, because people who don't understand satellite imagery are unlikely to use it.

The secrecy has also defeated those who kept the secrets. When arms control agreements were offered, politicians and voters, who were unaware of our capabilities, opposed controls. When others warned us about the Soviet threat, critics were skeptical because there wasn't any proof.

This book will try to plug this hole between the cursory magazine articles and the professional works. I have written it to appeal to:

Historians who want to know about the development of overhead imagery and how it affected the space program.

Members of the military who know about spy satellites, but don't know what they can see or how to avoid them.

Spy buffs who want to know how we gather much of our intelligence.

Businessmen and managers, who need to know how satellite imagery can help them.

Students who are learning about career possibilities.

Civil libertarians, who need to know the threat satellite imagery poses and how to protect themselves.

Voters and politicians who want to know where the tax money went, how satellite surveillance keeps the peace, wins wars, and verifies treaties.

Police and investigators who want to know how to use satellite photography.

The curious who just want to know more about satellites and what they can do.

In order to satisfy all these, I've covered a broad field: history, how satellites work, how they are used, how you can use them, and where to buy the imagery. Although sketchy in many places, I've tried to bring a person to a level where he can make intelligent decisions about using satellite imagery. I hope the book is as much fun to read as it was to write.

Part I

How Satellites Work

1

The
Evolution of
Overhead Photography

The concept of overhead photography was born long before the airplane or camera, or even the balloon. Leonardo da Vinci had a fascination with pictures, flight, and military matters that would have made him a natural photo interpreter. In the early 1700s, people like Dr. Brook Taylor and J.H. Lambert wrote about optics and how the principles of perspective could be used to produce photographs. However, the theory had to wait until the problems of flight and photography were solved.

Soon after the daguerreotype was developed by Louis Daguerre in 1839, people realized the possible use of cameras and lighter-than-air craft in mapping. The first to understand this was Colonel Aim'e Laussedat, who, in 1849, tried to take aerial photographs from kites. He had so many problems that he reverted to terrestrial methods, but his work earned him the title of Father of Photogrammetry (photogrammetry is the measurement of information with photography).

The first known photograph taken from the air was taken in 1858 by a French photographer named Gaspard Felix Tournachon. He used a balloon to ascend 80 meters over the town of

Bievre, France, for this photograph. This success encouraged other photographers and soon balloon photography became popular with the French.

Aerial photography arrived in time to be a part of the first of the modern wars, the Civil War. General George McClellan used captive balloons to photograph and map Confederate positions in Northern Virginia. Of course, each innovation inspires a countermove, so McClellan's balloons inspired some unknown Confederate artilleryman to invent anti-aircraft fire. In the early days of the war, a Union balloon was observing enemy positions from what is today the Balston Metro Station. This obviously didn't please the Confederates, near what is now Seven Corners Mall in Falls Church, so they raised the barrel of their gun and let fly at the target. From that humble beginning came a new branch of warfare.

The end of the Civil War relegated aerial photography to peaceful purposes. In 1882, kites were used to obtain photographs for meteorological uses. In 1906, they were used to photograph the damage caused by the San Francisco earthquake.

By this time, another innovation appeared — the aircraft. In 1909, a photographer accompanied Wilbur Wright in an aircraft in Centocelli, Italy, while Wright was training Italian Naval Officers, and took the first photographs from this new platform.

The high ground became important in the trench warfare of World War One. Although the balloon was the first platform for cameras, it was soon surpassed by the biplane. The cameras were bulky and often were just hand-held by the observer, but they proved their worth in the static warfare of Europe.

It wasn't until World War Two that the true worth of overhead photography was recognized. The US went into the war with the crudest knowledge of aerial photography and interpretation, and within five years leap-frogged past the British to take the lead as the world's best overhead photographers and interpreters. That lead was to become critical in what was to become the greatest challenge in America's military history — penetrating the Iron Curtain.

After WWII was over, the USSR became the threat. Unfortunately, the Soviet Union was a closed society under Stalin, and travel by Soviet citizens and America's military attaches' was restricted and most of the intelligence we needed was unavailable. The US needed a way to look inside.

Figure 1-1

Before the U-2, modified bombers, such as this Canberra RB-58, were used to gather intelligence within the USSR's borders. Note the camera window below the word "AIR." (Photograph by Harold Hough.)

The first intelligence efforts used captured German aerial photographs from WWII. These were supplemented by aircraft that skirted the USSR and took photographs as far as 100 miles inside the border. (See Figure 1-1.) Obviously, these were risky flights and, over a decade, more than 40 aircraft and 200 airmen were lost to Soviet anti-aircraft fire.

As valuable as this information was, the USSR was a large country and photographing targets from outside the border allowed us to see only a small portion of it. Unfortunately, US intelligence didn't have any alternatives, since our spy networks behind the Iron Curtain were riddled with Communist informants, and agents were being captured with sickening regularity.

The first attempt to fly over the USSR was with weather balloons (GENETRIX program). These craft carried cameras and were sent aloft into the jet stream. There they would take photographs as they traveled across the USSR. Then they would be recovered after the trip. This was a failure. Most of the balloons were shot down by the Soviets and those few that were recovered provided very little intelligence. However, the GENETRIX project had one benefit: the cameras developed for this program were the basis for the first satellite cameras.

By 1953, America's concern with the USSR had become a panic. The Soviets exploded their first hydrogen bomb and May Day parades were showing new jet bombers. Could the Russians be preparing a massive bomber fleet to attack the US? The Eisenhower administration needed to know and only overhead photographs could provide the answers.

The solution came from the bastion of America's secret projects, Lockheed's Skunkworks in California. Under the direction of CIA officer Richard Bissel, Lockheed built a revolutionary aircraft that could fly higher than Soviet aircraft or missiles — the U-2.

The U-2 was the first major intelligence coup of the post-WWII era. It could fly at about 80,000 feet, higher than most engineers thought an aircraft could operate. It also could glide considerable distances. In one instance, a U-2 had a flame-out during a training flight over Tennessee, yet it managed to glide to Albuquerque, New Mexico. Combined with these technical feats was a 4,000 mm camera that could see objects just a few inches in diameter from 80,000 feet up. Yet, with the large area the camera covered, just 12 flights of the U-2 could photograph the whole land mass of the US.

The U-2 made its first operational flight on July 4, 1956, from Wiesbaden, Germany. Since US intelligence felt the first flight had the element of surprise working for it, the plane was given the task of flying over the heavily defended cities of Moscow and Leningrad. The flight was a major success. Within a few months, Eisenhower knew that the USSR didn't pose a major threat with its bombers.

The Soviet bomber threat was replaced by the missile threat when the USSR launched Sputnik. As the US fell far behind in the race for space, the Eisenhower administration needed to know the threat the Soviet missiles posed in order to judge the proper response. Thanks to the U-2, Eisenhower soon knew the missiles weren't a major threat and he refused to increase defense spending, despite the public outcry. It was the U-2 that was responsible for keeping the budget balanced so long.

Soviet missile improvements caused two concerns. Photographs were confirming US fears that the USSR would soon be able to produce missiles that could strike the US. At the same time, the improvements in missile technology also meant the high-flying U-2 was in greater risk from Soviet surface-to-air missiles. For the Eisenhower administration, however, it was the concern about the possibility of operational missiles threatening the US that forced the president to order the U-2 over three Soviet missile sites one last time.

On May 1, 1960, pilot Francis Gary Powers took off from an airbase in Pakistan. His goal was to photograph three Soviet missile facilities in Tyuratam, Sverdlovsk, and Plesetsk before landing in Bodo, Norway. The flight over Tyuratam went off without a problem, but a Soviet missile hit him over Sverdlovsk.

Powers survived the attack, and he and the aircraft gave the USSR a major propaganda story.

At first the US denied it was spying and insisted the aircraft was just a high-altitude research plane from NASA. This story was clearly wrong and the government finally admitted it was spying on the USSR. The results were catastrophic and the Paris Summit, held two weeks later, was a disaster. In an attempt to placate the Soviets, Eisenhower promised Krushchev that the US would suspend U-2 flights over the Soviet Union. The Iron Curtain had closed once again.

Reconnaissance in Space

"I wouldn't want to be quoted on this, but we've spent 35 to 40 billion dollars on the space program. And if nothing else had come out of it except the knowledge we've gained from space photography, it would be worth 10 times what the whole program cost. Because tonight we know how many missiles the enemy has and, it turned out, our guesses were way off."

— President Lyndon Johnson

Eisenhower's promise to discontinue U-2 flights over the Soviet Union was a calculated gamble and an attempt to limit future public relations damage. He succeeded at both. The uproar about spying died down and within 100 days America was once again spying on Soviet missile installations. Only those privy to the US's attempt to put a spy satellite in space knew how much Ike had risked by discontinuing the U-2 flights, because America's space program had been a disaster.

The US spy satellite program was born nearly 15 years before the success of the first prototype, Discoverer XIII. A report by the Douglas Aircraft think tank, Project RAND, on May 2,

1946, stated the technology from the German V-2 could put a satellite in orbit. Although it listed many civilian uses for these craft, it stated, "It should also be remarked, that the satellite offers an observation aircraft which cannot be brought down by an enemy who has not mastered similar techniques."

Figure 1-2

The replacement for the U-2 was the SR-71 Blackbird. Unlike Power's U-2, this aircraft could fly higher and faster than any surface-to-air missile. (Photograph by Harold Hough.)

With the onset of the Cold War, this function became more important for the US Air Force. They not only needed information on targeting, they also needed reports on cloud formations and weather over the USSR, in case of a war. The Defense Department commissioned more reports on the applicability of satellites for reconnaissance.

Further study suggested three possible methods for spying over the USSR. The first alternative was to take photographs with a camera and recover the film. This was rejected because it was too bulky, limited by the amount of film, and required a method for recovering film from space.

The second method was to take photographs with conventional film, and then transmit the photos to the ground by television. This also appeared impractical, because it was still limited by film and, at that time, it took about 45 minutes to transmit a photograph, while the satellite would only be in contact with a ground station for about 10 minutes.

The third, and most practical, option was to use a television camera in space and broadcast the images back to the ground. This offered "real-time" intelligence and was simpler than the other systems. Unfortunately, televisions of that time offered poor resolution and the smallest object the satellite could detect would have been 100 feet in diameter. This was too small for finding anything on the ground, but it interested the Air Force because it was good enough for extracting weather information. As a result, work started on this type of satellite. It lead to the TIROS class of satellites, made weather forecasting a more accurate science, and provided the first tangible benefit to the US population.

Obviously, the most practical system couldn't provide any valuable intelligence, so an alternative was needed. After considerable bickering, the US decided a recoverable film package was the most practical and could be put in space the fastest. While development continued on each of the systems, the greatest effort was put into orbiting a camera and retrieving the film. In 1958, Eisenhower approved Project CORONA and decided to use the Discoverer satellite program as the cover story for the work. The program manager for this effort was Richard Bissell, the same one who successfully directed the U-2 construction.

The CORONA spy satellite was to be launched into a 150 by 240 kilometer orbit for 17 orbits. After receiving a command from Kodiak, Alaska, it was to eject its film canister, which would reenter the atmosphere. While it was parachuting down, an Air Force plane would recover it in mid-air. The film was then to be returned to Washington, DC.

Launching and recovering a film canister proved to be harder than originally thought. The first twelve Discoverer missions were failures. (Although Discoverer II did successfully eject its film, it landed near the Norwegian/Soviet border and was probably retrieved by the USSR.) Evidently, one of the problems was keeping the satellite and its equipment warm in space. The problem was solved by applying tape to the skin of the satellite so it could absorb heat from the sun.

Success finally came to the Discoverer/CORONA program on August 10, 1960 when Discoverer XIII was finally launched and recovered. Although there wasn't a camera (the payload was a package of sensors that recorded the flight), it did have a device that allowed US intelligence to learn if Soviet radar was tracking the satellite.

Just a week after Discoverer XIII, the CIA launched Discoverer XIV with a modified camera from the failed balloon project of a few years earlier. It was recovered and, for the first time, the US had satellite photographs. The satellite had photographed Mys-Schmidta air base and the ICBM complex at Plesetsk (the same target Francis Gary Powers was trying to photograph when he was shot down). The resolution was poor, only about 50 feet, but to Andrew Goodpaster they were "like the dog that walks on its hind legs, remarkable that it happens at all." However, the first step had been made and, as the scientists improved the system, the photos became better.

While the Discoverer/CORONA was providing a wealth of information, another project, SAMOS, was turning into a failure. SAMOS was the project that took photographs and then transmitted the images to earth electronically. The first satellites were successfully launched a few months after the success of the CORONA program, but they proved to be a total failure. The images were poor and interpreters couldn't even decide if the pictures were of Russia or China. As a result, the project was cancelled in 1962 and CORONA became the father of the US spy satellite program.

Looking Through The Keyhole

Where scientists and intelligence officers lead, security bureaucrats follow. The success of the CORONA program meant new security procedures and codewords. The new code name for the reconnaissance satellites was KEYHOLE, usually abbreviated to KH. The first camera system used was designated KH-1, the second KH-2, and so forth.

Once the bugs were worked out of the Discoverer/CORONA program, the CIA designed the satellite to carry two film capsules so the US had longer coverage and the number of launches was limited. This satellite still fell under the CORONA program, but was designated the KH-4A. It was first successfully launched in May, 1963, and a total of 46 were sent up in the next four years.

The next improvement of the spy satellite came in 1966 with the KH-4B. Although it was similar to the KH-4A, the camera was improved and the resolution was four times as good. It was first launched in August, 1966, and there were 33 successful launches over the next 6 years.

Although the KH-4 provided valuable information, the resolution of 10 feet wasn't good enough for many intelligence missions. As a result, the US built a "close-up" satellite called the KH-7 (code name GAMBIT). This class of satellite orbited about 20 miles lower than the KH-4, and, with a better camera system, it could provide a resolution of about 18 inches. The only problem was that the camera was fixed and could only shoot targets directly under the spacecraft. This was a problem that scientists would rectify in future systems.

The KH-8 was the next class of spy satellite, and one of the most successful, in that it supported US intelligence efforts for two decades. It was first launched in July, 1966, and the last one flew in 1984. Like the KH-7, it was a close-up satellite that flew even lower than its predecessor. It also had improved optics and was the first satellite that provided color photographs, even though the resolution was worse than the black and white photos it provided.

The KH-9 represented the marriage of the wide area coverage of the KH-4 and the resolution of the KH-7 and KH-8. It also had several modifications that made intelligence gathering easier. Some film was sensitive to infrared in order to detect camouflage. It also had 4 film canisters, to allow a longer mission life. It was first launched in June, 1971, and the last successful mission was in June, 1984. A total of 19 missions were launched and many operated for over half a year. Ironically, the only failure was in 1986, when it exploded soon after take-off. In some ways, this was its most important mission, since the US had been nearly blinded by a string of rocket failures, including the space shuttle.

While all these satellites were providing excellent intelligence about the Soviet Union and its missiles, they were a failure in other ways. They hadn't provided any indications about the Arab/Israeli wars of 1967 and 1973 or the Soviet invasion of Czechoslovakia in 1968. Although the US was tracking events, especially in the case of the 1967 war, the time lag between when the film was exposed and when it was recovered was critical. In each of these cases, the previous photos showed nothing of concern, while the next set of photos (while excellent) arrived in Washington too late to be of any use.

Although the SAMOS project and a test television camera on the KH-9 were failures, US intelligence had to return to the concept of a "real-time" satellite. Unfortunately, the TV tube wasn't good enough, so they went after another technology, the charged coupled device. The CCD (as it's called) was first discovered in the 1960s by Bell Labs and offered better resolution and flexibility than the conventional TV tube.

This invention allowed the development of the most recent spy satellite, the KH-11. The KH-11 was first launched during the final days of President Ford's term and became operational on Carter's first day in office. Unlike its diminutive predecessors, the KH-11 is a monster weighing about 30,000 pounds, 64 feet long, and 10 feet in diameter. Thanks to its improved optics, it could orbit higher while still providing better pictures. This allows it to stay in orbit longer. In fact, this is the first spy satellite that stays in orbit for years. It was first launched in December, 1976, and is still the US's main spy satellite, even though it has undergone many modifications.

The most recent modification of the KH-11 was launched on August 8, 1989, by the shuttle Columbia. Although called the KH-12 by the press because of its modifications, the military calls it Advanced KENNAN or Improved CRYSTAL. Unlike its predecessor, it can also see infrared with its sensors, which allows it to see targets in the dark or items that produce heat. The resolution of the infrared viewer isn't as good as the one that views visible light, but it adds a capability that wasn't available earlier.

The real time capability of the KH-11 finally proved its worth nearly thirty years to the day after the successful launch of Discoverer XIV. In late July and early August, 1990, the KH-11 noted Iraqi troop movements along the Kuwaiti border. When Iraq attacked on August 2, President Bush, who had been involved in the development of the KH-11 as the Director of Central Intelligence, had advance warning. Although the spy satellite will have many more improvements, it has finally met the expectations put on it half a century ago.

Commercial Satellites

Commercial satellites have always been the stepsisters of the military reconnaissance satellites. Not only have commercial systems been forced to use less sophisticated optics, but in many cases their capabilities have been limited by the intelligence community. In fact, in 1962, President Kennedy created an inter-agency committee to study the political aspects of America's spy satellites. One of the suggestions of the committee was to limit future civilian satellite resolution to no less than 98 feet. The recommendation was accepted and even 30 years later, US LANDSAT images still can't see anything smaller than that (although competition from the USSR and France is forcing the newest LANDSAT satellite to improve).

In the beginning, the lower resolution was acceptable. One of the first civilian applications of overhead imagery was with the lunar orbiter and the moon mapping program. Because the orbit was lower and there wasn't any atmosphere to ruin the images, NASA used the KH-5 camera system.

As more and more photos from manned space missions were made public (obviously these weren't from the purely military missions that astronauts made and are still making), scientists saw more civilian applications. As a result, the US initiated the Earth Resources Technology Satellites Program (ERTS) in 1967. The first satellite, ERTS-1, was launched in 1972, onboard a Nimbus weather satellite. What was special about this system, was that the satellite recorded information from several spectral regions, not just visible light (green, red, and blue).

The success of the ERTS program led to the launching or four more satellites (now called LANDSAT). The latest satellites can detect 7 different bands of light and have a resolution of 30 meters. Plans call for the 1991 launch of LANDSAT 6 with a sensor capable of seeing objects as small as 15 meters.

Thanks to the commercial systems, satellite data are now available to the average person. For as little as a few hundred dollars you can buy imagery from nearly anywhere in the world. In later chapters we will go into what is available and how to acquire it.

The US LANDSAT program isn't the only commercial satellite image system. The satellite with the best digital resolution is the SPOT (Satellite Pour l'Observation de la Terra) satellite launched by the French. It has a resolution of 10 meters and can see 4 bands of light with its sensors. Until the SPOT was launched in 1986, the US government had grown "fat and happy" with their product. Since SPOT has appeared, LAND-SAT is improving its resolution and service. Now the satellite image business has become more customer oriented.

The final player in the commercial satellite business is the USSR. Two former military satellite systems, the KFA-1000 and the MK-4 are used to produce photographic products (unlike the electrical images of LANDSAT and SPOT). Although they don't offer the flexibility of the French and US systems, the Soviet photos have the best resolution (5 meters) and they can be used without a computer.

Summary

Overhead imagery has advanced considerably, especially since Discoverer XIV returned over 30 years ago. Most of the growth has occurred in military intelligence instead of civilian or scientific applications. While the military has had unlimited budgets, the civilian sector has been forced to work with obsolete equipment and within the strictures of intelligence guidelines. While this has limited some peaceful applications, we will see later in the book that the civilians later took the unsophisticated systems and developed uses and methods the intelligence community hadn't imagined.

2

Fundamentals
of
Satellite Imaging

Don't let the words "imaging" and "remote sensing" scare you. Although they are often used by professionals in describing satellites, both imaging and remote sensing are used on earth. For instance, imaging is the process of producing any image, whether it's produced with film or electronics (like a TV camera). Remote sensing is just the principle of detecting something from a distance. When we walk into our kitchen and see the electric element of a stove glowing red, we know it's hot. That's remote sensing. We detect the radiant heat on our skin and we see the glowing red metal and we know that these two signs usually indicate heat. Direct sensing on the other hand, occurs when a 5-year-old walks into the kitchen, touches the stove and burns himself. Obviously, he isn't an expert in remote sensing.

Like remote sensing, the principles behind imaging satellites aren't very much different from what we are familiar with. Whether it's a billion dollar spy satellite system, a ten dollar disposable camera, or a thousand dollar video camera, the principles are basically the same. If you can understand how the

$10 camera works, you can understand the most sophisticated spy satellite.

The process of imaging starts when light is reflected from an object towards the camera. It passes through a lens (or a pinhole in early cameras) that focuses the light so it appears at the back of the camera as an image. The place where the image appears is the focal plane and that's where the film or the electronic sensors are located. (See Figure 2-1).

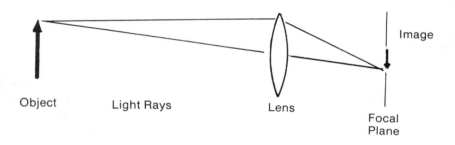

Object   Light Rays   Lens

Image

Focal
Plane

Figure 2-1

All cameras operate on the simple principle of using a lens to focus light onto the focal plane, where the image is captured on film and transmitted electronically.

One of the most critical elements in the imaging system is the lens. Early cameras used a small pinhole that allowed only a small amount of light to reach the film. Unfortunately, the amount of light was so small and early film was so insensitive to light, that it could take hours for an image to appear. The first photograph, taken in 1827 by Joseph Niepce, took about 8 hours.

By adding a simple lens and a shutter, more light could hit the film in a shorter amount of time. At the same time it made photography easier because photographers found lenses could change the perspective of the image. Like telescopes, some lenses could make distant objects appear close and others could allow the photographer to take panoramic photographs.

The telephotos had a problem. The more powerful they were, the longer the lens. There were two solutions. The first was to add more elements in order to shorten the length. This added more glass and weight to the lens, but kept the size down. Another solution was to fold the light path with mirrors so it wasn't as large. Although it has limitations, it used less glass (the more glass, the less resolution) and was lighter. As a result, most satellites rely less on lenses and more on mirrors to gather and focus the light.

The electronics revolution changed the way we detect and record images. Obviously, before the TV camera the only way to register an image was with light-sensitive film. The light would enter the camera and strike the silver compounds in the film. When the photons hit the silver halide crystals, they would change chemically. During development, these altered crystals were turned into silver while the rest of the unexposed chemicals were washed away.

The photographic method was simple, inexpensive, and offered high resolution. Although it didn't offer the "real time" of a television camera, they were much more valuable. It wasn't until the charged coupled device arrived in the 1970s that a realistic alternative to photographic film came. Although not as sharp as film, the CCD offers some advantages that aren't available with the photographic method.

In the electronic camera, the CCDs replace the film on the focal plane. Instead of striking the silver halide crystals, the photons strike the individual CCDs in a grid. The signals from the devices are recorded and can be processed later (we will talk more about CCDs in the next chapter).

We now have covered the basics of most remote sensing devices,whether they are spy satellites sensing a Soviet surface-to-air missile site or a camera sensing a beautiful girl. The light reflected from the object is collected through a lens or mirrors and then is detected by film or electrical devices on the focal plane. The information is then stored by developing the film or transferring the electrical impulses to a computer.

"If these expensive spy satellites are similar to a commercial camera," you ask, "why don't we just send up commercial cameras with the astronauts and save the rest of the money?" Good question. The fact is, NASA and the Department of Defense have sent commercial cameras with astronauts to take military photographs since the early 1960s. That's one reason why the DOD is always interested in a manned space station.

But commercial cameras can't detect many different types of light. In fact, unless it uses infrared film, the regular camera can only discern what you can observe with your eyes. The fact is, there is a lot more out there to see.

When I described a remote sensing device earlier, I said light bounced off the object, passed through the lens, and struck the sensors. I didn't mention the importance of the type of light shining on the object, the type of light the object absorbed, and whether or not the object was emitting its own light (like a light bulb). As you remember from your schooling (if they still teach such things in today's schools), the light we see is only a part of the electromagnetic spectrum. Depending on the wavelength, the energy can be seen or a sophisticated detector is needed. The smallest wavelengths are cosmic rays and x-rays. From .4 to .7 microns the energy is visible. From .7 micrometers and up, the energy is infrared, then microwave, and finally radio and TV waves. Out of all this energy, only the visible light and segments of the infrared spectrum can be recorded on film. The rest requires sophisticated devices.

Does the type of light reflected matter? You bet it does. In our example of the kitchen stove, we would have assumed the stove was cold if we didn't detect infrared energy on our skin and a red color through our eyes. If the element wasn't red, we would have moved our hand close to the element in order to detect lower levels of energy. If the palm of our hand didn't detect anything, we would finally resort to direct sensing (touching it). What would your reaction have been if the element was green? The fact is, the type of light we receive makes a difference.

We first applied our knowledge of different types of light to find camouflage. In World War Two, infrared film was used to detect the difference between foliage (which reflects infrared light) and camouflage (which usually absorbs infrared light). The principle that the type of light received in the camera can mean totally different things is still used today to detect everything from military units to mineral deposits.

By looking at the different types of light received by the imager, we can learn what is reflected from the object, what is absorbed by the object and what is emitted by the object. Of course, first you must know what type of light is shining on the object. If, for instance, a powerful green light is directed towards a tree during the fall, it may still look green because that is the only type of light that can be reflected from it.

Fortunately, we have an advantage because we can determine the type of light shining on an object. If we photograph an object during daylight, we know how much ultraviolet, blue, infrared, etc., is being received by the object. Then, by recording the light reflected from the object, we can determine some of its characteristics. Now, let's look at what can happen to light and how we can identify objects from outer space.

Light and Satellites

Although we don't think about it, all objects above absolute zero radiate energy, and this includes living things. (You were right when you told that girl she was radiant.) As you read this book, you are bombarding the environment with microwaves and other electromagnetic energy that would make a Luddite or rabid environmentalist sick. (And to think, your mother didn't file an environmental impact statement when you were born.)

Of course, the hotter the object, the more energy is radiated and the shorter the wavelength. When an object reaches about 1000 degrees Kelvin (0 degrees Kelvin is absolute zero and 273.16 degrees K is 0 degrees Celsius) or 726 degrees Celsius, the wavelength becomes short enough to become visible to the naked eye. As the object becomes hotter, the color changes until it becomes white.

If we know the temperature of the object, we can determine the predominant type of light it's emitting. The equation is: wavelength = 2898/object temperature (Kelvin). Therefore, if you want to know what type of light a human body radiates, you divide 2898 by the 310 (the temperature of the body in Kelvin). The answer is 9.348 microns, which is part of the thermal infrared spectrum. Therefore, humans primarily emit infrared radiation, although they also radiate small amounts of microwaves.

The sun acts in the same way as a hot human body. The only difference is that the sun's temperature is about 5,700 degrees Celsius. At that temperature, most of the energy radiated is in the visible part of the electromagnetic spectrum, although it still radiates ultraviolet, infrared, microwave, and other bands of energy (see Figure 2-2).

Since we can mathematically determine the type of energy radiated by the sun, we should be able to determine the characteristics of an object that reflects only certain types of light. Not necessarily. Although the sun radiates a broad band of energy, only a certain percentage of it makes it to earth and then back to the satellite in space, because the atmosphere often blocks light. How and why it effects energy is just as important to remote sensing as our sensor because it determines how we want to build our detector and how we use it.

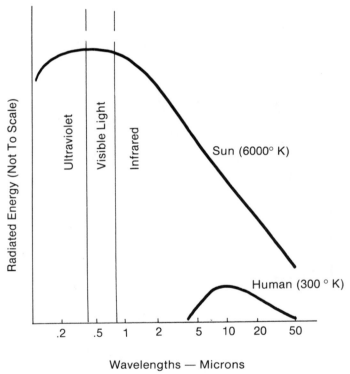

Wavelengths — Microns

Figure 2-2

Most of the energy radiated by the sun is in the visible portion of the spectrum. Most of the energy radiated by a human body is in the infrared portion of the spectrum.

How the Atmosphere Effects Energy

Everyone knows the earth's ozone layer blocks ultraviolet waves. However, the atmosphere also blocks other types of energy (see Figure 2-3) while letting other light in nearly unimpeded. Obviously, a sensor tuned to one of the absorbed wavelengths will be ineffectual, so most remote sensing, especially that from satellites, must be made in the areas that have the best transmission. These areas are called windows and later you will see that these windows correspond directly with the bands that satellites such as the LANDSAT view.

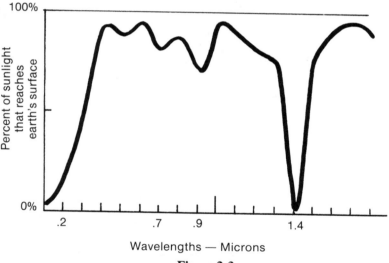

Figure 2-3

The Earth's atmosphere blocks certain wavelengths of light while allowing other wavelengths to pass through.

One of the major effects of the atmosphere is scattering caused by the particles and molecules in the air. The predominant scattering is called Rayleigh scatter. This occurs when light interacts with molecules and small particles in the air. This scattering happens in shorter wavelengths, such as ultraviolet and blue energy, rather than long waves, such as red. It's Rayleigh scatter that accounts for the blue sky, because the blue light from the sun is reflected about the sky by the atmosphere and literally comes from all directions, not just the sun. If there wasn't Rayleigh scatter, the sky would appear black and the only light from the sky would come directly from the sun.

Rayleigh scatter is the chief culprit responsible for the blue haze we see when we look at objects far away from us. This haze represents the scatter occurring between the object and the observer. As a result, the objects aren't as crisp and you have to compensate for this or use the red light band because it doesn't scatter.

Rayleigh scatter is also responsible for dramatic sunsets. As the sun sets, the light must pass through a larger portion of the atmosphere and the effect of the scatter becomes more pronounced. In this case, not only is the blue eliminated, but also the green. Only the remaining red light is left to paint the sky and the clouds. Rayleigh scatter may hinder ultraviolet and blue light, but we are more than compensated by the wonderful sunsets it gives us.

Another type of scatter is called Mie scatter. This occurs when the wavelength and the particles in the air are the same size. This is more pronounced on overcast days when the particles or the water vapor in the air reduces clarity.

Another problem is nonselective scatter, caused when particles larger than the wavelength are found in the air (usually water particles). Unlike the other types of scatter, this obstructs all visible and infrared light equally and can't be effectively penetrated with any band of light. Since it scatters all light equally, the result is white. That's why clouds and fog are white.

Atmospheric Absorption

Until now, we have talked about how particles or molecules scatter light energy. However, if you remember your science classes, you know all elements absorb certain types of energy. The science is called spectrography, and with it, you can identify unknown compounds.

The same principle holds for the atmosphere and its compounds. Certain molecules, like ozone, carbon dioxide, and water vapor, absorb energy in the ultraviolet and infrared parts of the spectrum. As a result, whole bands of light are prevented from reaching the earth's surface, even though the sun produces sufficient quantities of that energy. The remaining bands of light that pass through the atmosphere are called windows.

We now have all the elements required to determine what a satellite should look at. If you look at Figure 2-4, you see the type of energy that the sun produces, the type of light that passes through the atmosphere, the compounds that interfere with light transmission, and the type of sensors that can detect the energy. Obviously, some windows are in parts of the spectrum where there is little energy from the sun, so even though the transmission is good, there is little information to record. On the other hand, there are areas of the spectrum where sunlight is plentiful, but transmission is poor. As a result, the best places to look are in only about half a dozen windows where light is plentiful. This is, in fact, where the LANDSAT satellite looks. Of course, one band (band 6) is where there is little solar energy, but we can see objects there because, as we mentioned earlier, all objects warmer than absolute zero radiate energy and that band corresponds to the band of energy radiated by the earth and other objects of about the same temperature (such as people).

We have now discussed the four key factors in remote sensing — the sensor, the light source, how light reacts with the object, and how light reacts with the atmosphere. By simply knowing what to look for and noting what we find, we can learn as much about an object from 200 miles in space as if we were only a mile away.

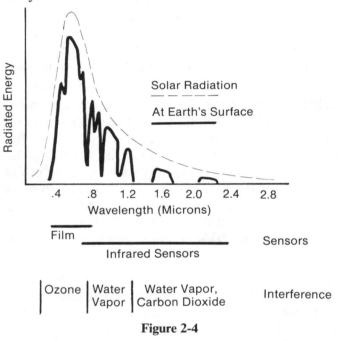

Figure 2-4

The amount of information that can be captured by sensors is determined by the amount of energy radiated, the interference with that radiation, and the type of sensor used.

Resolution

Gathering the light into the sensor is only the first step in a long process. You have to manipulate and interpret the information so it can be useful. But how good is the information?

Everything has a benchmark for measuring performance. In automobiles, it's the time to go from zero to sixty. In fighter aircraft, it's what speed it can reach. In satellite imagery, it's resolution. There are many other measures, but it's the resolution of a system that sticks in people's minds.

So, what's resolution? It's the smallest object that can be seen in an image. Obviously, the finer the resolution, the more information that can be extracted from the image. And, despite what you may think, commercial equipment in space can provide a level of resolution that would give a civil libertarian heebie jeebies.

Resolution can be easily determined for any system with the following formula. Resolution = (Distance/focal length) X resolution diameter. Resolution diameter is the size of the light-sensing element in the system, whether it's a CCD or film. In the case of film, resolution is usually stated in terms of lines per mm. That means the film has enough resolution to show that many separate parallel lines in one mm of negative. While the standard for commercial film is around 100 lines per mm, high resolution film like Kodak's Technical Pan have resolutions over 300 lines per mm.

Using the formula above, let's see what the resolution of a satellite could be if we used readily available equipment. If we put a 35 mm camera on a satellite that had an orbit of 150 kilometers and used a commercially available 1,000 mm lens and Kodak Technical Pan film, the equation for resolution would look like this: (150 kilometers/1,000 mm) x .000003 mm = .45 meters. That means commercially available equipment costing about $1,000 could see something as small as 18 inches in diameter, about the size of second base! Of course, this is theoretical resolution. Actual resolution will be affected by the atmosphere.

Of course, just because you have resolution good enough to see something doesn't mean you can tell what it is. If someone stole second base (literally) and put it in the middle of a parking lot, the interpreter couldn't tell the difference between that and a white shopping bag that someone had thrown out of their window. On the other hand, if second base is on a baseball field, along with all the other bases, the pitcher's mound, and the baselines, the interpreter would be able to identify it with certainty.

Resolution is also affected by contrast. A polar bear on a field of snow would still be hard to see despite the resolution of 18 inches. On the other hand, an object that stood out from its background or even reflected light differently could be seen. For instance, a signal mirror, just the size of a credit card, could be seen from space if it reflected the sunlight properly. As we said earlier, remote sensing is more than sensing; it also concerns how the light interacts with the object. That's why resolution isn't everything and why looking at different bands of light can be just as important.

Satellites

So far we've discussed the basics of sensors, light energy, and resolution. Now let's look at the spacecraft and what it takes to operate the sensors properly. During the early days of satellite reconnaissance, the military learned more was required than launching a satellite in orbit to take pictures. Equipment needed energy to transmit and stay warm, and the early solar cells were expensive and inefficient. It took several years and many failures before the equipment operated reliably.

One of the major problems was maintaining the satellite's stability. All satellites tend to tumble in space, just as even a well aligned car will inevitably go off a straight road if no one touches the steering wheel. When that happened, the camera might very well be pointing at the stars instead of the earth when the camera was operating.

The solution required small rockets to stabilize the spacecraft. However, it was hard to keep the camera pointed down when there wasn't any gravity to tell which direction was down. The first solution was to have the satellite find the horizon on both sides of the earth by looking for the difference in temperature between space and the earth. That method worked well for years and was finally superseded by systems that look at stars for guidance. These keep the satellite properly oriented and are more accurate.

Other problems with satellite imagery were covering the whole earth and providing consistently high quality photographs. Manned missions and many other satellites travel around the earth on an equatorial path, going west to east. Unfortunately, that limits photography to the areas around the equator, a liability to any imaging satellite, especially one spying on the Soviets.

The solution is a polar orbit, where the spacecraft passes over the north and south poles on each orbit. During each orbit, the earth's rotation makes the satellite pass about 2700 kilometers west of the previous orbit (in the case of LANDSAT). This gradual procession across the face of the globe serves two purposes. The first is that it allows the satellite to cover the entire globe. The second is that it allows the satellite to follow the sun. This gives all the images a similar amount of sunlight for consistency. It also allows the spacecraft to pass overhead during the mid-morning when the atmosphere is clearer and shadows don't obstruct the view.

After gathering the data, the final problem is returning the information to earth. Today, digital information can be stored on board until the satellite comes in range of a ground station or it can be transmitted "real-time" via communications satellites from anywhere in orbit. Obviously, this latter method is used with the KH-11 spacecraft.

One final innovation has made satellite imagery more responsive. While the polar orbit allows each part of the earth to be viewed every couple of weeks, rapidly changing events (like wars) may necessitate more frequent viewing. Many modern satellites like the KH-11 and SPOT have "off nadir" viewing. This allows the sensors to view objects hundreds of miles off track by rotating a mirror so it can look sideways. As a result, one satellite can view the same area every few days instead of only a couple of times a month.

Summary

Satellite imagery and remote sensing are complex fields and mastering them requires experience in several disciplines, such as orbital mechanics, physics, and optics. However, if you remember that everything depends on how light reacts with the target and how the image is received and manipulated, satellite imagery won't be mysterious and will be something you can use in your work.

3

Satellite
Sensing Systems

In the previous chapter, I said imaging satellites were comparable to cameras. In some cases, that's just what they are. However, recent advances in electronics have provided engineers with other options than just photographic film. Let's look at some of the sensors seen on satellites, how they work, their advantages and disadvantages.

Photography

The reported demise of silver-based photographic film has been greatly exaggerated. Despite claims that conventional photography is doomed to obsolescence, it's still actively used in space-based imagery. In fact, it has several advantages over its more sophisticated cousins.

Simplicity

No other imaging system is as simple as photography. The satellite doesn't need extensive electrical systems to store images or transmit data. Nor does it require a large solar array to power the systems. As a result, with fewer systems, there are fewer things that can fail and reliability is improved.

High Resolution

The smallest sensing element in film is the silver halide grain. In high resolution film, the grains can be as small as .05 microns. Although intelligence agencies won't tell us what the size of their CCDs in photo reconnaissance satellites are, they probably are 30 times larger. Therefore, with the same optical system, film will always have greater theoretical resolution. (See Figure 3-1.)

Figure 3-1

Photographic surveillance has many advantages over non-photographic methods. This Soviet image of Washington, D.C. has excellent resolution of 15 feet. (Photo courtesy Central Trading System.)

Size

A film camera system is smaller than an electronic system with all the necessary solar cells, and electronics.

Cost

As I mentioned in the last chapter, commercial equipment can provide surprising resolution for thousands of dollars, instead of millions.

Simpler Interpretation

For those readers who plan to use satellite imagery on a shoe-string budget, photos are the cheapest alternative. They are cheaper to buy and you don't need a sophisticated computer for interpretation. In fact, all you need is a good magnifying lens.

As a result of these advantages, traditional photography is still being used extensively on Soviet satellites and manned missions. However, it does have limitations which have relegated it to a minor role in space imagery. Some problems are as follows:

Time Lag

As US intelligence discovered in the 1960s and 1970s, good images aren't enough when they prove to be too late to act on. It always takes time to photograph, retrieve, and develop the film, so it can't be used for fast-moving events like wars.

Sees Less

As I mentioned earlier, there is much to be learned by observing other, invisible, parts of the electromagnetic spectrum. Unfortunately, film can only see blue, green, red, and infrared. These limitations make it less desirable for many applications in geology.

Less Opportunity To Interpret

Computers are powerful tools for enhancement and interpretation. As a result, electronic data are more useful for sophisticated interpretation. Conventional photographs can only be interpreted with conventional methods, unless the user digitizes the image.

Needs More Light

Conventional film needs more light than modern electronic sensors. As a result, photographs are only available during daytime. This may not be a hindrance for the commercial user, but military interpreters are paranoid and like to see what the enemy is doing at night.

There are only two sources for photographic images from space. The United States offers images from manned flights, through EROS. Unfortunately, the coverage is poor and these images are best used as decorations for the office, instead of interpretation.

The best source for photographic images is the Soviet Union. The Soviets use black and white film that's sensitive to specific parts of the spectrum. This offers better resolution than color film and allows the user to look at discrete frequencies much as you would do with LANDSAT or SPOT images.

The Soviet cameras work much like conventional ones. The MK 4 camera has a 300 mm lens and each negative is 18 x 18 cm in size. They are launched for 25-day missions and photograph whatever ground control orders.

After the mission is completed, retrorockets slow the spacecraft and the descent module separates from the rest of the craft. The module lands by parachute and the film is processed while the cameras that were recovered are used in a future flight.

Since the best images come from the original negative, all orders are sent to the USSR, where the negative is used to fill the request. As a result, it may take longer to acquire the image you want, but the resolution makes it worth the wait.

Electronic Imaging

Despite the dramatic resolution of film, space imaging belongs to electronic devices. Since the early days of photo reconnaissance, there has been a need for "real-time" images. Conventional television cameras used too much energy for satellite solar cells and they didn't have good resolution.

One of the first solutions was a return beam vidicon (RBV). The RBV had a camera-like shutter and exposed a photosensitive plate to the light. Then a raster beam read the image and sent the data back to earth. Although the resolution wasn't good enough for many military purposes, the 80 meter definition made it a valuable tool for earth resource management.

Multispectral Scanners

One solution to the poor resolution of television cameras and the limited sensitivity of photographic film was the multispectral scanner. Despite the electronics revolution of the 1970s, this system is one of the most popular satellite imaging systems even a generation after its first application in space. In fact, most satellite imagery users still prefer this type of information to the finer resolution of the CCD.

The multispectral scanner is basically one system that can scan many different parts of the electromagnetic spectrum. As we mentioned earlier, different types of light can provide us with different types of information about a target. Consequently, it immediately has an advantage over photographic systems.

Figure 3-2 shows the basic components of a multispectral scanner. Light from the earth enters the spacecraft and hits a rotating mirror that scans a line perpendicular to the path of the satellite. The light is split into the different wavelengths by prisms or dichroic grating. (See Figure 3-3.) Each separate band is then read by a separate detector. The computer then interrogates the sensor regularly (usually thousands of times a second). The information from each sensor is then processed electronically. Usually the information is given a digital value that corresponds to the amount of light energy received. In the case of current LANDSAT models, that's a number from 0 to 255, with 255 as the strongest signal. The information is then stored or transmitted to earth.

Figure 3-2

A multispectral scanner from the LANDSAT 6 Thermatic Mapper. In the center are two black chips for detecting bands 5 and 7. The device just to the right of the chips is a thermal infrared (band 6) detector. The whole scanner is about the size of a quarter.

The multispectral scanner has several advantages. Not only can it detect more types of energy, but, by using a mirror, it can scan large areas while still only using just one sensor. Of course, image resolution is a function of the spacecraft's speed and the rotation of the mirror. In addition, the process of scanning while the satellite moves means the images aren't geometrically true and distortions occur. However, the type of information available, and the fact that computers can correct for distortion and some poor resolution, makes the information popular with many scientists.

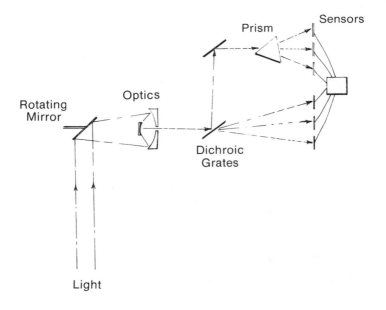

Figure 3-3

Light enters a multispectral scanner from a rotating mirror, where it is divided by wavelength and recorded by sensors.

Charged Coupled Devices

Imagine a checker board with a shot glass in each square, and you have a good idea of the latest in solid-state imaging devices, the charged coupled device. The CCD, as it is called, is the heart of the latest spy satellites, the key to the French SPOT satellite's resolution, and the reason the newest home video cameras can operate in low-light conditions.

The CCD is a grid of small, light-detecting semiconductors, some only about a micron in diameter. (See Figure 3-4.) In reality, they are much like the shot glasses in our example. They collect any photons that fall on them and store them until needed.

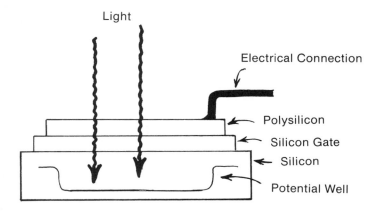

Figure 3-4

A CCD element works by transmitting an electrical charge relative to the amount of light captured and stored.

As the photons hit the element, they build up an electrical charge in the semiconductor. When a computer orders the CCD to empty its charge, the first row of sensors passes its charge into a waiting shift register, like someone emptying the shot glasses in the first row into a set of waiting glasses. As the first row is passing its charge to the shift register, the second row is passing its charge to the first row and so forth. The data from the second row (now in the first row) is then passed into another awaiting shift register.

The information from the CCDs is passed to a CCD controller, which labels the position of each of the charges in the overall picture and measures the electrical charge on a scale of 0 to 255 (other scales are used, but 0 to 255 is standard for 8-bit converters). The information can be stored or transmitted to earth.

CCDs offer more than instant images and resolution. Unlike film, which only uses about 2% of the light that strikes it, CCDs convert as much as 80% of the light into a signal. In photographers' language, that means CCDs have an effective speed of ASA/ISO of over 100,000! Therefore, they can capture images in low-light situations or take "moving pictures."

CCDs do have their problems. They can't capture as many bands of energy as multispectral scanners (just visible and near infrared), so they aren't as effective in sophisticated earth resource studies. They also become sensitive to a low-level current called dark current. Although this isn't critical in normal situations, this current can interfere with the legitimate electrical signals and subtly change the image. This is usually countered by cooling the CCD with a thermoelectric cooler or liquid gas.

CCD technology is new and still advancing. As scientists find ways to make them sensitive to more parts of the electromagnetic spectrum, they will inevitably sweep the multispectral scanner into the dustbin of history.

Radar

While ozone, water, and methane molecules absorb energy from certain parts of the visible and infrared spectrum, the atmosphere is relatively transparent to microwave energy (commonly called radar). Therefore, they can see through many types of haze and clouds that would hinder our view. But that's only part of the attraction of spaceborne radar. It also has other advantages that interest civilians and military alike.

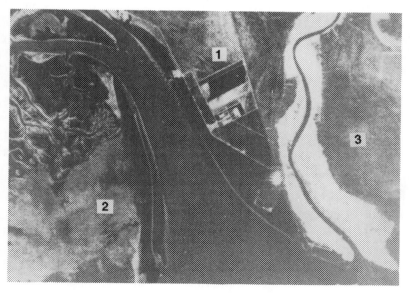

Figure 3-5

A radar image of parts of Iraq and Kuwait. Number 1 is an Iraqi oil terminal at the mouth of the Shatt al 'Arab. Number 2 is a Kuwaiti island. The bright reflections near Number 3 are caused by date palms lining the banks of the river.

Nighttime Capability

Since radar usually transmits its own signal, observation isn't limited to sunlight. This is obviously a benefit to the military intelligence community, which wants to track the enemy at night or under cloud cover. That's why the US has the LACROSSE satellite, which uses radar to see under clouds. According to reports, it has a resolution of three to five feet.

Radar Provides Different Information Than Visible or Infrared Light

Microwaves can give the observer an opportunity to learn the roughness of the ground, its electrical characteristics, and even physical characteristics of the vegetation.

Radar Can See Some Subsurface Features

When the conditions are right, radar can see through the surface (like a dry sand) and detect the bedrock, even if it's a few meters underground. Spaceborne radar can also detect submerged enemy submarines.

With all of these advantages, it's easy to see why radar data are often used along with other types of satellite imagery.

How Radar Works

Until now, all the systems I've talked about are just fancy cameras. Obviously, radar is different. Unlike the other systems that passively receive energy reflected from the sun or emitted from the object, radar broadcasts pulses of microwave energy in a particular direction and then records the strength and delay of the reflected energy.

The spacecraft broadcasts a short microwave signal perpendicular to the direction of travel. It then measures the time until the signal returns (which indicates the distance from the target to the satellite) and the strength of the return (which indicates the brightness of the image pixel). That information is processed by a computer and the information can then be turned into an image of the terrain.

The resolution of satellite radar systems depends on two factors, pulse length and antenna beam width. A long micro-wave pulse allows objects close to each other to reflect energy back to the antenna at the same time. Consequently, the radar can't differentiate between them. As a result, the best resolution is provided by a short burst that allows the radar and operator to identify each object.

Antenna beam width is the amount the microwave signal spreads out as it travels. Obviously, the more the beam spreads, the more likely two objects the same distance away from the satellite will be mistakenly identified as the same object.

Of course, the beam width is related to the wavelength of the pulse and the size of the antenna. In this case, the longer the antenna is in relation to the wavelength, the better the resolution. Unfortunately, in the case of a spacecraft, an effective antenna could be longer than the satellite itself.

The solution to this dilemma is the synthetic aperture radar. As the satellite travels through space, its short antenna acts like a long antenna, receiving data over a period of time. Consequently, an antenna just a couple of meters long can act like an antenna over a kilometer long!

When the antenna receives the return signal, it not only records strength and time, it also measures the shift in frequency (known as the Doppler effect). If the microwave beam spreads apart and hits an object slightly ahead of the satellite's position, the Doppler effect pushes the frequency up (the opposite, if it's behind the craft). By measuring the frequency and accounting for it, a computer can process the information in such a way as to make the effective beam width very small and improve the resolution.

Resolution of radar images can be improved by using a focused synthetic aperture radar. In that case, the resolution is one half of the actual antenna length. Therefore, the resolution of the satellite with a two meter antenna would be one meter, no matter how far in space it was placed (of course, the further away, the weaker the signal).

Why Radar Is Useful

Radar has two characteristics that make it a valuable tool for satellite imagery. The first characteristic makes the shape of the target an important consideration in the type and strength of a signal reflection. For instance, if a satellite takes a radar image of a mountain (see Figure 3-6), the side towards the spacecraft will provide a strong image while the side away from the satellite may provide a weak or nonexistent return. This explains the strong highlighting in some radar images. Another type of strong image return is the corner reflector. An example is the street that reflects the radar beam into a building, which sends a strong return directly back towards the satellite. In cases like that, even objects smaller than the radar's resolution can be seen.

Radar can also detect texture in the object, depending on the frequency used. If the object's surface has a roughness equal to or larger than the wavelength of the microwave signal, the object acts like a diffuse reflector and the image received by the spacecraft shows a rough texture. If for instance, an object has ripples that are 5 cm from crest to crest, a 10 cm radar signal would show a smooth surface while a 3 cm radar signal would show a rough surface.

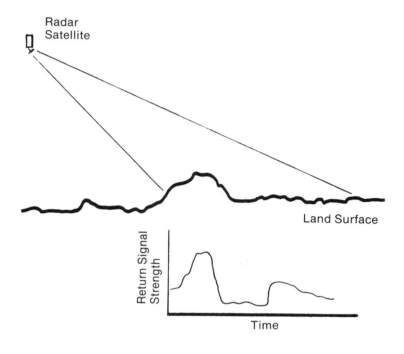

Figure 3-6

A radar image of a mountain exaggerates the difference between the mountain and the surrounding terrain.

If the microwave beam is polarized, like a light passing through a polarizing filter, the scientist can see if the roughness is random or has a pattern. If the object is rippled (like a potato chip), polarized microwave signals and the polarization of the return would indicate which directions the ripples ran. This is useful in oceanic studies because radar can closely monitor the pattern of waves. In fact, the Navy devotes considerable effort to radar satellites because they know a submarine can disturb the wave pattern.

The strength of a returning signal is also determined by the conductivity of the object. This is called the dielectric constant and the higher the constant, the better the signal. Since dry soil has a low dielectric constant and water has a very high one, radar can monitor water content in the soil. If the sand is extremely dry, the radar signal may even pass through it and reflect off the bedrock below it.

By combining the ability to see water content and surface texture, radar can also study vegetation. Since leaves contain water and have a large surface area, radar can detect different types of crops and the characteristics of the vegetation canopy.

Passive Radar

Another imaging technique used in satellites is passive radar. Although it's not as well known in civilian circles, it's used by the military. It can operate without giving itself away (unlike conventional systems that transmit microwave signals) and it can even detect stealth aircraft.

As I mentioned in the previous chapter, everything with a temperature above 0 degrees Kelvin radiates energy. The only difference is the quantity of energy radiated and the length of the waves. In the case of objects on earth, most of the energy is found in the infrared part of the spectrum. However, there is a small amount of microwave energy radiated in nature (not enough to cook a TV dinner though).

These low level radiations, as well as any reflected or transmitted microwave energy from other sources, such as the atmosphere or other objects can be detected with a sensitive radiometer. Like conventional units, passive radar can detect dielectric constants and texture.

Passive radar is a stepson of radio astronomy, sensing stellar objects with radar receivers. Since sensitivity is important when receiving a weak signal, passive radars use an internal temperature reference source to correlate the signals received and the signals expected from the ambient temperature. The difference between the reference signal and the incoming signal is then stored. Obviously, the weak signal means the antenna are larger and spacial resolution is less than with conventional units.

Since a passive radar isn't actively seeking out targets with a transmission, the unit can only record what is received by the antenna. However, if the antenna is moving in a spacecraft (or other object) and the antenna is sweeping back and forth across the path of the satellite, the unit can make an image of the ground, based on the radar images. These images have many of the characteristics of radar, but don't attract the attention of the enemy. They are also good for detecting hot, high conductivity objects (such as aircraft or tanks) and can see through thin layers of soil to give an idea of the underground structure. Since all objects radiate some energy, these radars can even detect weak signals from stealth aircraft or other radar absorbing objects. Unfortunately, as long as passive radar has such important military applications, the civilian sector will remain relatively ignorant of the advantages of this technology.

4

Enhancing
Satellite Images

Putting a camera or sensor up in space and retrieving the image is only the first step in making satellite images. The difficult work is done back on earth.

The images return to space as a stream of digital signals. These signals tell the receiving station the value of each pixel in the image. In most cases that value ranges between 0 and 255, with 255 as pure white and 0 as black. In the examples in this chapter, we will use a smaller scale with 0 as black and 9 as pure white. An actual image with a 0-9 scale wouldn't have the shades of grey or the fine resolution of actual images, but it will make the process simpler to understand.

When the data is sent back to earth and processed, it can be displayed on a monitor. Each piece of data from a CCD or a sensor is assigned to a pixel on the TV screen (if you look at most modern TV screens, you can see the individual pixel elements). If the original value from the satellite assigned a value of 0 to that pixel, the screen shows black. If the value was 255, the pixel is white. All the numbers between are shades of grey ranging from very dark to nearly pure white. The result is a black and white image of what the satellite saw in space.

Using our 0 to 9 scale, the information on a monitor would look like Figure 4-1. In this case the picture would be of a black cross on a white background.

9	9	0	9	9			6	6	5	6	6
9	9	0	9	9			6	6	5	6	6
0	0	0	0	0			5	5	5	5	5
9	9	0	9	9			6	6	5	6	6
9	9	0	9	9			6	6	5	6	6

Figure 4-1   **Figure 4-2**

Figure 4-1 and Figure 4-2

Figure 4-1 represents the stark contrast of a black cross on a white field, while in Figure 4-2, both cross and field are similar shades of grey.

Unfortunately, most data doesn't appear as clear as the cross. In many cases, the object of interest and the background are both shades of grey as in Figure 4-2. Although we can tell from the values that it's still the cross, the image on the computer monitor would be indistinct.

In order to make the data easier to visualize, analysts can manipulate the data so objects stand out from the background. This technique is called enhancement.

Since satellite imaging equipment is designed to detect every-thing from dark land forms to bright sunlit snow, the sensors are very flexible. However, in most cases, the information from one scene covers only a part of the 255 values available to it.

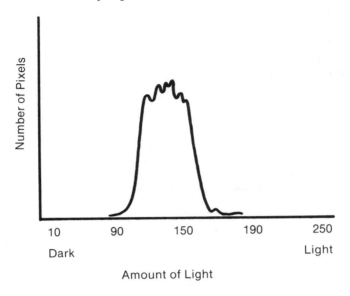

Figure 4-3

This graph depicts the original information captured by a satellite. It is difficult to interpret because it is so bunched-up.

In Figure 4-3, we see a graph of an image. The darkest pixel has a value of 80 and the brightest one is 200. Most of the values can be found between 110 and 170. If this was displayed on a monitor, the image would be a muddy grey and it would be difficult to separate objects from the background.

The simplest solution is to stretch the contrast by manipulating the values. In Figure 4-4, we took the original value of the pixel, subtracted 80, and multiplied it by 2. Now the pixel values are stretched between 0 and 240 and the contrast in the image has improved. This uniform stretching of the information is called a linear stretch.

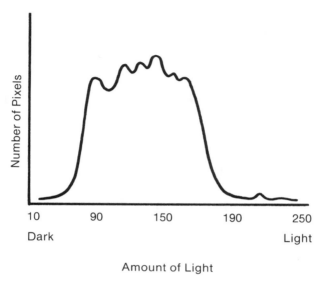

Figure 4-4

Using a technique called "stretching," the information in Figure 4-3 is spread out to provide more contrast, making it easier to interpret.

One problem with the linear stretch is that it assigns values to every pixel in the image, even if there are few pixels of that value. For instance, there are few pixels with values of less than 30 and more than 230. So we could stretch the values more and make all the pixels smaller than 30 black (value of 0) and those over 230 white (value of 255). This adds more contrast to the image, further defines more important parts of the image, and eliminates unusual sensor readings (caused by a glitch in the equipment or transmission) called artifacts.

Another stretch technique is called a histogram stretch. Since most of the information is found between 140 and 165, you can stretch that part of the information over a greater part of the 255 values to provide greater detail while disregarding the rest of the information.

You can also use special stretch techniques if you want to emphasize a certain feature like water or forest. In that case, you would give more of the 255 values to those tones you want to study and relegate the rest of the shades to the remaining values.

In the case of the image in Figure 4-2, we can stretch it out by subtracting 5 from each pixel and then multiplying by 9. Then the image would have the same contrast as Figure 4-1. That is the linear stretch.

Edge Enhancement

5	5	6	5	5			5	5	7	5	5
5	5	6	5	5			5	5	7	5	5
5	5	6	5	5			5	5	7	5	5
5	5	6	5	5			5	5	7	5	5
5	5	6	5	5			5	5	7	5	5

Figure 4-5   **Figure 4-6**

Figure 4-5 and Figure 4-6

Edge enhancement increases contrast. The vertical line in Figure 4-5 is easier to see when enhanced in Figure 4-6.

Since the images are taken from space, the resolution is never as good as the interpreter would want. One way to sharpen the image is by enhancing edges. This makes it easier for interpreters to notice objects that may be important.

Figure 4-5 shows a grey line in a grey field. When viewing this image on a monitor, it would be easy for the interpreter to miss it. One way to highlight the difference would be to compare the value of each pixel with its neighbors and then double the difference. By applying that technique to Figure 4-5, we come up with a better contrast in Figure 4-6.

Smoothing

Sometimes the information in an image is too confusing. In that case, the interpreter may want to eliminate some information by smoothing. This eliminates some sudden changes in image intensity and makes the image easier to view.

5	5	5	5	5
5	5	5	5	5
5	5	6	5	5
5	5	5	5	5
5	5	5	5	5

Figure 4-7

5	5	5	5	5
5	5	5	5	5
5	5	5	5	5
5	5	5	5	5
5	5	5	5	5

Figure 4-8

Figure 4-7 and Figure 4-8

Smoothing eliminates minor differences in an image so that they do not distract from the main contrast. The slight variation in the center of Figure 4-7 is eliminated in the smoothed Figure 4-8.

In Figure 4-7, we see one pixel slightly different from the others. If we employ a smoothing filter, the computer will replace each pixel value with an average of it set and the surrounding 8 pixels. When that occurs, the different value is eliminated and the whole scene is just one shade of grey (as shown in Figure 4-8).

Sometimes the image received is distorted because of the satellite's optics or the atmosphere. With the help of the computer, we can correct for it. If the optics are distorted, then all the images can be processed through one formula to eliminate the problem. The solution is more complicated if the atmosphere causes the trouble. The different temperatures in the atmosphere can distort the light waves just like a hot road distorts light passing over it, giving rise to watery mirages.

5	8	5	5	5		5	8	5	5	5
5	8	5	5	5		5	8	5	5	5
5	8	5	2	2		5	8	5	2	2
8	5	2	2	5		5	8	5	2	2
5	8	5	2	2		5	8	5	2	2

Figure 4-9   **Figure 4-10**

Figure 4-9 and Figure 4-10

The image in Figure 4-9 is distorted. When corrected in Figure 4-10, it reveals a straight line (road and a rectangle football field).

If there is a point of reference on the ground (such as an object of known shape and dimensions), interpreters can make corrections. In the case of Figure 4-9, we know the group of 2s in the lower right hand corner should be a rectangular football field, however temperature variations distorted the middle of the field. By accounting for that lateral distortion and moving the image back into shape, we now can see in Figure 4-10 that the road on the left hand side is really straight, not curved.

If there isn't a reference on the ground, satellites can make their own corrections by bouncing laser beams off the ground or measuring the curve of the wave lengths. This method is called "active optics.".

All the enhancement techniques we've discussed improve the shape and definition of the objects viewed. They're called spacial enhancement techniques. However, they can't find everything. For instance, if we're looking for a camouflaged tank in a forest, these methods won't help us. That's when we need spectral enhancement.

Spectral Enhancement

Shape is important to interpreting objects, but the type of light it absorbs and reflects can reveal more. For instance, both the forest and the camouflaged tank reflect green light. However, as we mentioned earlier, plants reflect more infrared light than camouflage does. (See Figure 4-11.) So if we looked at an image of the infrared part of the spectrum, the tank would stand out.

Sometimes, however, we want to include more than just one type of light in our image. If for instance, the tank and forest were near a town, we might want to look at red light because red is the one visible band not affected by scatter.

The easiest way to include more than one band of light in an image is to make a color composite. The most common one is the true-color image where the information from the blue part of the spectrum is given a blue color, green is green, and red is red. The resulting picture then looks much like it does from overhead.

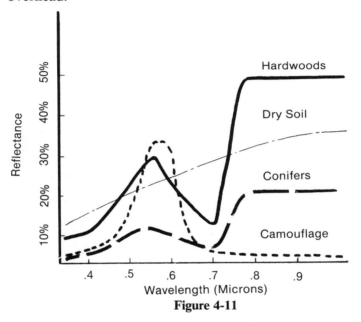

Figure 4-11

Different materials reflect more or less of each band of light, helping interpreters distinguish features in satellite images.

A true-color image would show the buildings in our tank and forest image, but it wouldn't help show where the tank was hidden. Since we aren't using the green part of the image very much, we could take the information from the infrared band and assign it the green values on the TV. The result would be an image that would show the buildings (red), the tank (red), and the forest (green, since plants reflect more infrared). This is called a color infrared picture (and we will discuss it in a later chapter).

Color images make interpreting easier, but sometimes that still isn't enough. A color image can only show three colors (red, green, and blue) while there are as many as seven bands of light recorded by the LANDSAT satellite. Moreover, the information can be confusing. As a result, scientists have developed many methods for combining different types of information and displaying it so more information can be displayed in a more understandable manner.

Coordinate Transformations

Spectral analysis does more than just study the types of light reflected from objects. It can also assist in spacial analysis. For instance, a strong shadow in an image could either hide an important object or even be highlighted in the enhancement process. However if we look at the ratio of light reflected in each band instead of the gross amount of light reflected, the shadow becomes less important and it becomes possible to ignore it or even find something in its shadow.

When using more than one band of light, it's important to make the right selection, because much of the information shown in one band is the same as other bands. For instance, with LANDSAT imagery, the seven bands fall into 4 categories: visible light, near-infrared, mid-infrared, and far-infrared (thermal). Each of these categories tends to show the same information. For instance, something that is visible to the red band is probably going to show in the green or blue band. Consequently, when you're trying to extract the most information, it makes sense to use just one band of information from each of these categories.

As careful as you try to be, there will always be some confusion when you blend bands. For instance, one type of light might highlight a crop of oats growing in a field while another band highlights a field of wheat nearby. If you just combine them, both fields will be highlighted and the interpreter will be unable to differentiate them.

One way to eliminate confusing pictures, where two or more objects have the same brightness, is to make one object lighter than the surrounding area and the other object darker. This way, the information in each of the objects is unique to itself and can't be confused. The enhancement method used is called a co-ordinate transformation. It's called a coordinate transformation because the coordinates are the brightness values of the pixels and they are transformed into new values.

4	4	5	5	5		5	5	5	5	5
4	4	5	5	5		5	5	5	5	5
5	5	5	5	5		5	5	5	5	5
5	5	5	5	5		5	5	5	4	4
5	5	5	5	5		5	5	5	4	4

Figure 4-12

-1	-1	0	0	0
-1	-1	0	0	0
0	0	0	0	0
0	0	0	1	1
0	0	0	1	1

Figure 4-13

Figure 4-14

Figure 4-12, Figure 4-13, and Figure 4-14

In "coordinate transformation," the values of one band (Figure 4-13) are subtracted from the values of another band (Figure 4-12) to create an image that has more contrast (Figure 4-14).

We can see a coordinate transformation in Figures 4-12, 4-13, and 4-14. Band A is Figure 4-12 and shows an object in the upper left-hand corner. Figure 4-13 is Band B and shows an object in the lower right-hand corner. If they were merely combined, the information from the objects in each corner would look the same and could confuse someone looking at them. However, by subtracting Band B from Band A (Figure 4-14), the object in the upper left-hand corner has a negative value and is darker than the background while the other object is lighter. With a simple mathematical manipulation, we can then make the one object black, the other one white, and the background a neutral grey.

Although we subtracted one value from another in this example, we can also divide A by B. That method is used when looking at vegetation because it provides more information and shows greater differences between plant types.

Principal Component

In a coordinate transformation, we just subtracted one image from another. If we looked at the formula of the enhancement technique, it would look like this:

(1.0) Band A + (-1.0) Band B = pixel value.

In coordinate transformations, the values in brackets are always one or a negative one. However, if you use values that don't equal one, you may be able to highlight more differences or objects. The numbers used are usually determined by making a graph of the distribution of pixel values in both of the bands (Figure 4-15). The value for Band A would be the cosine of the angle while the value for B would be the sine. Therefore if the angle was 20 degrees, the values would be .9397 and .3420 respectively.

The second principal component calculation switches the values and Band A uses the sine and B the cosine.

Since the principal component analysis is useful when studying the earth, scientists have developed a special set of principal component calculations especially useful for earth studies because they account for the way information is distributed among the light bands. This set of calculations is called Tassled Cap transformations. They are one of the more popular enhancement techniques used by interpreters to study the earth.

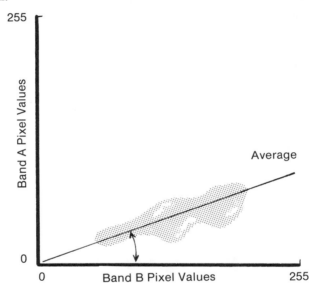

Figure 4-15

In "principal component analysis," the pixel values of Band A and Band B are graphed and averaged to get an angle which is used in adjusting the image to reveal more information.

Ratio Images

The ratio image is generated by comparing the information from two bands of energy and then displaying the ratio of the values. This is important in detecting subtle differences in rock formations, because it emphasizes the variance in the two bands.

It's also helpful because it isn't hindered by shadows or lighting differences that may occur over a whole scene. Therefore it can be very helpful in interpreting scenes with many clouds or mountains that cast long shadows.

In Figure 4-16, you can see how shadows from a couple of clouds have confused the images and varied the light reflected back to the sensor. Figure 4-17 (Band B) isn't any better and the only obvious correlation is in the dark areas in each image where the shadows are.

5	3	1	3	5			6	3	1	4	5
5	2	1	4	5			7	2	1	5	6
6	2	3	5	6			9	3	5	8	9
5	4	5	4	2			5	5	6	5	2
5	5	4	2	1			6	6	5	2	1

Figure 4-16   **Figure 4-17**

1	1	1	1	1
1	1	1	1	1
2	2	2	2	2
1	1	1	1	1
1	1	1	1	1

Figure 4-18

Figure 4-16, 4-17, and 4-18

The information provided in Figures 4-16 and 4-17 is confusing. When subjected to ratio analysis (Figure 4-18), an obvious pattern emerges.

However, when you look at the ratio of Band A to Band B in Figure 4-18 (for simplicity, I rounded the ratios to the nearest whole number), you can see a line running through the image that was hidden in both bands because of differing light and confusing reflections. The important clue to finding this object was that it reflected a greater amount of Band B light than the surrounding area.

Temporal Enhancement

Measuring the changes in a scene over time is a valuable enhancement technique, especially in intelligence applications where the opponent is trying to make changes without arousing attention. However, it can also be used to measure natural phenomena such as flooding, the movements of glaciers, and agriculture.

3	3	6	3	3		0	0	0	0	0
3	3	6	3	3		0	0	0	0	0
3	3	6	3	3		0	0	0	0	0
3	3	3	3	3		0	0	3	0	0
3	3	3	3	3		0	0	3	0	0

| **Figure 4-19** | | | | | | **Figure 4-21** | | | | |

3	3	6	3	3		3	3	6	3	3
3	3	6	3	3		3	3	6	3	3
3	3	6	3	3		3	3	6	3	3
3	3	6	3	3		3	3	9	3	3
3	3	6	3	3		3	3	9	3	3

| **Figure 4-20** | | | | | | **Figure 4-22** | | | | |

Figure 4-19, Figure 4-20, Figure 4-21, and Figure 4-22

"Temporal enhancement" highlights the changes to an area over time. The first image (Figure 4-19) is subtracted from the second image (Figure 4-20) to produce an image of the differences (Figure 4-21). Figure 4-22 shows how the differences are emphasized when Figure 4-21 is added to Figure 4-20.

Temporal enhancement requires two images from the same scene that can be accurately related to each other. One technique is to compare the images "side by side" by flickering the TV monitor between the two. This highlights major differences as they flicker on and off.

Although there are many methods for showing temporal changes, Figures 4-19 through 4-22 show one way. Figure 4-19 was taken of a road before it was fully completed. Figure 4-20 shows the completed road. If the first image is subtracted from the second image, the values seen in Figure 4-21 remain. If these values are then added to the second scene, an image remains (see Figure 4-22) that shows the road and the surrounding area, but highlights the newly built road by showing it in white.

Temporal enhancement techniques are an important part of automated change-detection. With this type of software, a computer can detect changes in an image and notify an interpreter so it can be reviewed manually.

Summary

As you can see, there are many possible enhancement techniques. When you change the combinations of light bands and the coefficients, you end with an infinite selection of possibilities. In theory, you could spend the rest of your life studying just one scene, yet learning little more about it.

Another problem with the various enhancement methods is the difficulty it poses to the interpreter of choosing which ones to use. The more combinations given to an interpreter, the more confusing the situation and the less probability that anything of value will be gained from the additional effort. As a result, unless the type of interpretation is unusual, most people involved with interpretation will stick to a handful of enhancement methods that provide consistent results and maximum information. In a later chapter, we will discuss how interpreters decide which methods will be the most valuable.

Part II

Uses
for
Satellite Imagery

5

Military
and Intelligence
Applications

In the first part of this book, we discussed the history of satellites and how they work. In this part of the book, I will show how this technology can be applied to many different fields.

The importance of America's spy satellites was demonstrated during the Senate debate on the 1987 Intermediate Nuclear Forces Treaty, signed by President Ronald Reagan and Soviet Premier Gorbachev. In order to convince Senator Boren and his Senate Intelligence Committee that the treaty was verifiable, Reagan had to promise to spend $12 billion to modernize the country's satellite reconnaissance fleet.

A couple of years later, when President George Bush was cutting the defense budget, the committee caught wind of an attempt to retreat on the promise and stretch the modernization over 15 years, instead of 5. Both the ranking Democratic and Republican Senators informed the National Security Adviser, Brent Scowcroft, that this was unacceptable and they would find other areas of the defense budget, such as personnel, to cut before they let reconnaissance satellites suffer.

Although spy satellites have been a critical part of verifying arms control agreements and tracking Soviet strategic weapons for nearly a generation, they have grown beyond that role. Real-time surveillance has allowed US intelligence agencies to expand their job. Modern satellites can take an image about every 5 seconds, and, with mirrors, can photograph images hundreds of miles off the track of their orbit. Since they don't have film to limit their operations, this has given the satellites many more applications. Today they are used for providing tactical information to military units, observing political events such as riots, and tracking military events in other critical countries such as those who sponsor terrorism.

COMIREX

Spy satellites come with their own bureaucracy, because there must be a method for deciding which targets should be viewed and which intelligence group will receive and interpret the data. Since there are several US intelligence agencies, including the CIA and the various branches of military intelligence, the infighting is controlled by handling all reconnaissance requirements through one impartial group. This group is called the Committee on Imaging Requirements and Exploitation (COMIREX).

COMIREX has members from most of the groups concerned with military reconnaissance and sets the priorities for determining targets. Then, when the images are returned to earth, the committee distributes the data and coordinates the responsibility for interpretation.

As with most Washington agencies, COMIREX isn't as important as the various groups that work under its umbrella. Groups like OPSCOM handle the daily operations, EXRAND tracks technological innovations and how they apply to reconnaissance, and KEYSCOM provides a library of images that interpreters can refer to. There are also other groups and programs that handle mapping and other intelligence requirements.

Any agency that needs satellite imagery must go through COMIREX. If the Navy needs photos of a new submarine in Sevastopol, they contact their COMIREX representative, who submits a request to the committee. The request lists the who, what, why, when, and where. The request can then be debated by the committee, depending on the number of requests before it and their importance. One tool for target selection is the automated management system called CAMS, which can help schedule the target, based on the agency's needs, other targets that must be photographed, and the orbit of the satellite.

Control of the satellite's product is made in Washington, but the satellite is actually controlled by the Consolidated Satellite Test Center HQ in Sunnyvale, California. A new center is being built in Colorado, however, because the current site is in a populated area and it's considered vulnerable to Soviet special forces attacks if we should go to war.

In the early 1990s, the Sunnyvale site controlled three major types of imaging satellites. The first is the KH-11, first launched in the 1970s. The next type is the Advance KENNAN, which is similar to the KH-11, but has better thermal imaging and mapping capability. The final satellite is the LACROSSE, which is a radar imaging satellite that can see under clouds and has a reported resolution of 3 feet.

Arms Control

It could easily be argued that spy satellites are the most expensive program the military has ever embarked on. Even the cost of the stealth aircraft program pales in comparison with the money spent on looking at the Soviets. Yet, despite all that money, there has never been a squeak from congressmen who would normally go into an epileptic fit at the most benign defense project.

Why not? Well, the large spy satellite budget is part of the defense and intelligence communities' black budget, and not made known to everyone. But the most important reason is the role played by spy satellites in keeping the peace for the last thirty years and helping the US and USSR achieve arms reductions by allowing both sides to verify compliance. Without them, SALT, START, and the INF would have been impossible.

In the summer of 1983, the US found out how important the KEYHOLE satellites were when they caught the Soviets violating the Anti-Ballistic Missile Treaty. An interpreter found a new ballistic missile detection radar under construction in Krasnoyarsk. Although such radars are allowed, the location and orientation was what was important.

The ABM treaty limited the US and the USSR to radars on the borders of their country. The purpose was to limit the effectiveness of any ABM system by limiting the amount of information available on the terminal phase of an ICBM's path. If radar was allowed inside the country, the ABM could better calculate the final target and have a better chance of intercepting the missile.

When this violation was made public, the Soviets denied any disregard for the treaty. According to them, it was a space tracking radar for their launch facilities in Plesetsk and Tyuratam. However, it was clear from the direction it was pointing, the radar couldn't track launches from their space centers. Instead, it was pointed to the northeast, where US submarine launched ballistic missiles would come from. After years of American pressure, the Soviets finally agreed to dismantle it in 1989.

Reconnaissance satellites do more than just look for illegal radar bases. Many of the key segments of any agreement must be verified by satellites (or other "national technical means," as they are often referred to). Just as important is the information they gather prior to treaty negotiations. Then they help negotiators learn what the Soviets are doing and what is verifiable with current technology.

Figure 5-1

Nuclear weapons storage compounds (A and B) at a Soviet military facility just north of Leningrad, as seen by LANDSAT. (Photo courtesy Autometrics and Earth Observation Satellite Corporation.)

One of the most critical aspects of arms agreements is numbers. It's up to satellites to photograph missile facilities and naval bases so interpreters can count missile silos, missile launchers, and ballistic missile submarines. (See Figures 5-1 and

5-2.) Obviously, the number of silos or submarines can affect the number of missiles counted, so arms agreements usually insist that empty silos or submarines have their covers removed so satellites can verify they are empty. The container is then destroyed so it can't be reloaded.

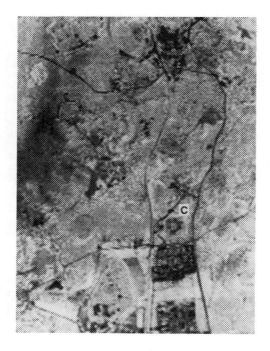

Figure 5-2

This is the same picture as Figure 5-1, made using different imaging techniques. The Star of David (C) is a sure indicator of a Soviet SAM site. Note how, in this image, the nuclear weapons storage compounds are almost invisible. (Photo courtesy Autometrics and Earth Observation Satellite Corporation.)

Another key aspect of arms verification is determining the types of missiles deployed. Current agreements only allow a certain number and type of modifications or new missile types.

Again, our agreements insist that changes in missiles be obvious from the outside (changes such as length or diameter, for instance). This makes them easier to see from space and often makes current launchers, submarines, or silos unable to handle them without modification.

One problem with spy satellites is that they can't determine if a missile has more than one warhead on it (MIRVed). As a result, the treaties assume that certain types of missiles are MIRVed whether the missiles actually have more than one nuclear warhead on them or not.

Part of arms control is seeing what the Soviets have deployed, but another part is determining what modifications are being made or what the status of new systems is. When a missile is launched from its test site, US spy satellites are tracking it every mile of the way. Reconnaissance satellites view the missile on its launch pad; signal intelligence satellites intercept the telemetry from the flight; and satellite images can view the impact to determine accuracy.

Arms control has grown beyond the agreements between the USSR and the US. We also watch developments of other nuclear nations, such as China, India, and Israel, to see what threats they pose. But the greatest interest is now being shown in the area of arms proliferation.

Keyhole satellites routinely collect information about other countries that are considered likely to make an atomic bomb. Countries such as South Africa, Iraq, Argentina, Brazil, Libya, North Korea, and Pakistan receive special attention from the US. Interpreters keep an eye on uranium mines, enrichment facilities, reactors, and research and development sites. This allows them to track progress, estimate the amount of nuclear material produced, and identify possible storage sites for completed bomb components.

But nuclear proliferation isn't the only concern. The US is also concerned about the development of ballistic missiles, chemical weapons, and biological agents. Suspect facilities are regularly monitored by the satellites and merged with information from other sources (such as high technology purchases) to determine the potential threat.

Changes in the last few years have shown that the USSR isn't the only threat. Therefore, more of the reconnaissance satellites' attention will be directed towards other nations and keeping other countries from gaining weapons of mass destruction.

Intelligence

In May 1984, an explosion wracked the weapons facilities in Severomorsk in the northern part of the Soviet Union. The explosion was so large that, at first, seismic recording devices in Norway and Sweden thought the USSR had detonated a nuclear weapon.

When the Keyhole satellite later flew overhead, they learned that about 1000 surface-to-surface and surface-to-air missiles had exploded, killing as many as 300 people. The damage was so severe that it affected the number of missiles the Northern Fleet could deploy.

By monitoring the aftermath of the explosion, US intelligence had a better idea of Soviet Naval capabilities in light of the damage to their inventory. Just as important, they learned that their initial estimates of the capacity of the warehouses were too low. In fact, original estimates had placed the total missile capacity at 200 instead of over a thousand.

Although this explosion was so noteworthy it made national news, photoanalysts are always making discoveries that affect our estimate of other nations' military strength.

The most obvious use of spy satellites in military intelligence is in detecting troop deployments and movements. Reconnaissance satellites can detect troop emplacements and even detect intentions by analyzing placement. If, for instance, the military is placed in defensive positions, that probably means an attack isn't planned. If, on the other hand, troop deployment has changed radically since the last images, equipment is placed near roads leading to the border, there is more activity, or new troops are in the area, there is a greater possibility that an attack is imminent.

Satellite images are even useful in a peacetime situation. By photographing maneuvers, or watching training facilities, intelligence specialists can determine military doctrine and how the units act under combat conditions. Careful study can even give insights into how the enemy might carry out an attack (or prepare a defense).

Satellites can also look at the ground, as well as the troops. With multispectral imaging, satellites can study the ground in order to determine if it can handle off-road military traffic or if it is too muddy to do so. They can also study road systems and determine choke points that should be bombed or captured. (See Figure 5-3.)

Of course, acquiring targeting information is one of the primary uses of spy satellites. If the satellite has an accurate mapping capability (as the newer Keyhole satellites do), mapping specialists can develop accurate coordinates for ICBMs or other weapons that require accurate placement.

One of the newer uses of mapping is in programming cruise missiles. Cruise missiles, such as the Tomahawk, use a sophisticated terrain-guidance system that finds the target by following the ground (a fancy "turn left at the hill and right at the river" system). With satellites, programmers were able to direct the cruise missiles towards their brilliant successes in Iraq.

Satellites are also able to determine future military power. By monitoring test facilities and research and development centers, analysts can learn about future developments in weapons. Then as new equipment is manufactured, they can track production levels at the factory and finally see the new equipment as it's shipped to the units in the field.

Figure 5-3

By manipulating this image of a military training facility (top), tank trails in the surrounding area become more visible (bottom). (Photo courtesy Autometric and Earth Observation Satellite Corporation.)

A well-known example of monitoring weapons development occurred when Samuel Morison leaked photographs of the

Soviets' first full-sized nuclear-powered aircraft carrier. Morison slipped these KH-11 photos to the defense publication *Jane's Defense Weekly*, where they were published. The US had been monitoring the construction for years and had based many of its predictions of future Soviet naval policy on this information. Ironically, the photographs told only part of the story and the analysts had picked the worst possible scenario. When construction progressed further, they learned that the ship didn't have the capabilities originally thought. That's one of the problems of overhead intelligence. There is always enough doubt for analysts to interpret the data in their own way.

A final use of satellites is to monitor events in a closed society. When Soviet troops fought Armenians or the Chinese attacked the students in Tienanmen Square, US satellites were watching from above.

Economic Intelligence

The military strength of any country is directly related to its economic power. As a result, satellites are often used to estimate economic conditions, especially in a closed society such as the Soviet Union.

One of the better known uses of satellite imagery is in estimating the size of the USSR's harvest. Each year, analysts look at the amount of land under cultivation, the health of the crops (more on this in the chapter on earth resources), and when farmers begin the harvest. From this, intelligence analysts have been able to develop accurate harvest reports that give us an insight into Soviet grain purchases.

In the Soviet Union, a bumper harvest isn't enough to guarantee adequate food supplies. Large percentages of the crops are often found rotting at the farms because transportation isn't available. This was the case in 1990, when the USSR had one of its best harvests, even though the nation was asking for food from other countries. One of the reasons for this contradiction could be found in satellite imagery.

In order to keep from dismantling much of its military hardware in Europe after conventional arms agreements were signed, the Soviet Army commandeered much of the nation's railroad capacity to transport the equipment across the Ural Mountains and out of the European theater. As a result, food never was shipped to places that needed it.

Reconnaissance satellites also look at factories and mines in many countries. By looking at the factory or mine, a trained analyst can often tell what is being produced. By measuring the size of storage tanks, the number of rail cars, and the size of the facilities, analysts can often determine how much is being produced.

Military Use of Commercial Satellites

Although they have their own fleet of satellites, the military often uses commercial satellites for intelligence purposes. The most obvious reason is to increase coverage. The US intelligence community has about 42,000 targets and it's hard to cover all of the them with the Keyhole satellites.

Although commercial resolution isn't nearly as good, there are still some missions it can handle, such as agricultural estimates. An analyst doesn't need to see each plant to make an intelligent guess about the potential harvest. In addition, the LANDSAT satellite has the ability to see many different types of light and is therefore an excellent choice for agricultural estimates.

The poor resolution of commercial satellites can also be used to monitor naval movements, missile base construction, or to develop maps. In 1990, US forces used LANDSAT imagery to update maps of Saudi Arabia prior to the war. The previous maps were made years ago by British cartographers and weren't accurate enough to fight a modern war. By using commercial satellite imagery, the military could reserve the Keyhole satellites for important missions such as photographing Iraq and Kuwait. LANDSAT imagery was also used to help pilots prepare for bombing missions in Iraq.

The military has also used commercial satellite imagery when they wanted to make something public, but didn't want to release a Keyhole image. In 1988, the Department of Defense used French SPOT images to show Dolon Airfield, a location for Soviet bombers, in the publication *Soviet Military Power.* This gave them the best of both worlds; Keyhole imagery remained secret, yet the American public was given an opportunity to see part of the Soviet threat.

LOCATION	REASON FOR TARGETING
Beloyarsk	Plutonium facilities
Cholyabinsk	Nuclear warhead assembly
Dnepropetrovsk	Missile production
Lokanga	Submarine fleet
Nikolayev	Ship construction
Novolitovsk	Ship construction
Plesetsk	Military launch and test facilities
Petropovlovsk	Fleet
Ramenskoye	Bomber test center
Sevastapol	Fleet
Severodvinsk	Delta and Typhoon Submarine production
Semipalatinsk	Nuclear underground testing
Sary Shagen	Star Wars R&D, Space tracking
Troitsk	Uranium enrichment
Tyuratam	Spacecraft launch facilities
Vladimirovka	Cruise missile testing
Vladivostok	Fleet

Figure 5-4

Likely Soviet targets for U.S. keyhole satellites.

6

Law Enforcement and Private Party Surveillance

When George Orwell wrote the novel *1984*, he envisioned a TV camera in every room spying on the occupants. Whether we like it or not, that time is here. Although we don't have cameras in every room, there are eyes in space that help the government enforce laws and can even tell if we water our lawns too much.

Depending on its needs, the government can either use the commercial or military satellites. Civilian use of military satellites started in 1967 when a study by the director of the CIA approved a method for sharing imagery with civilian concerns. In 1976, at the suggestion of the Rockefeller Commission study, the Committee for Civil Applications of Classified Overhead Photography of the US was formed to handle civilian applications. They act as a liaison between various agencies and COMIREX, which determines priorities.

Access to Keyhole imagery is limited to civilians who have top secret clearances and the agencies must be able to store such sensitive materials. As a result, few groups have regular access to spy satellites. A few agencies that use Keyhole intelligence are the FBI, the Drug Enforcement Agency, Customs, and the EPA.

Even though most government agencies don't have access to the military satellites, they are using civilian satellites in increasing numbers. Because the cost may range from a few hundred to a few thousand dollars, valuable information is becoming available to even some of the smallest departments.

Taxes

Governments need tax money to survive, so it makes sense that one of the applications for satellite imagery is in tax assessment. Of course, there are limits to its usefulness (it wouldn't be useful for monitoring sales tax), but it has many applications in tracking large assets, such as real estate, or income that is related to large tangible objects.

Overhead imagery has already been used in assessing property taxes. In large areas, property tax assessors can't hope to track all home improvements, so they need a source of information to tell them where the improvements are being made. The most obvious source is building or improvement permits filed by the owners. However, many people don't apply for permits because they want to avoid the paperwork or because they want to avoid higher tax assessments.

At first glance, civilian satellite imagery would appear to be too poor for detecting all but the largest buildings, because LANDSAT has a resolution of 90 feet, and SPOT, of 30 feet. Many houses are smaller than 90 feet and most renovations either don't change the size of the building or make additions that are much smaller than 30 feet.

What's more important than resolution, however, is the reflection. That's why roads smaller than the satellite's resolution are easily seen. The same principle applies to buildings.

For example, a homeowner in the suburbs decides to build a two car garage onto his house. The garage will be 30 feet square and will be added to a house that's 75 feet by 50 feet. The plot is 90 feet by 125 feet, so according to the resolution of LANDSAT, the property should be the smallest object the satellite can detect. Yet, the reflection of the land can give away the construction of the garage.

Before the garage is built, 3,750 square feet of a total of 11,250 square feet in the lot are covered by construction. The rest of the area (67%) is covered with grass, which is a strong infrared reflector. However, after the garage is built, 4,650 square feet will be covered by construction so only about 60% will be reflecting infrared (a 10% decline). Therefore, if before and after satellite images were compared, the later image would not reflect as much infrared. Although the image wouldn't show the construction itself, the change in reflections would give the tax assessor a hint that something is being built. In fact, by using a temporal enhancement technique, a tax assessor's office could find all the suspicious areas in the county and then dispatch assessors to see if any improvements have been made.

There is one caveat to using this method. The infrared reflectance of plants varies according to the time of year, the care, and the amount of water they receive. Therefore, it's nearly a sure bet the reflectance won't be the same as the previous picture. However, if you use some ratio imaging techniques, you can eliminate some differences. Just don't be surprised if you visit a lot expecting to see a shiny new building but only learn that the owner just stopped watering the grass.

Satellite imagery can also be used to verify income figures from farmers. As we will discuss in the next chapter, multispectral imagery can give analysts a good idea of crop yields, so tax officials can multiply yields by acreage and estimate future income. This can be used to verify tax returns, but the most useful application would be to use the information to estimate farm income for a region. This could become a base for determining future tax revenues or the economic health of the area.

Satellite imagery can also be merged with other tax information. For instance, the Census Bureau sells income information of areas (called TIGER). Commercial software allows the user to merge a satellite image of an area with this information in order to produce an income map of an area. It won't be too long before tax assessors combine income information with property improvements so they can spend more time targeting the rich than the poor.

Government Services

A storm ravages a state. Communications are disrupted. Travel is restricted because roads are underwater. The governor needs to assess the damage and see which places need help first. Rather than take a publicity-crazed tour of the damaged areas, why not use satellite photos? The images will show just as much (Keyhole images have been used in natural disasters), the governor can see more of the damage more quickly, and the images can be shown to more people.

Satellite imagery is good for more than just tax collecting and law enforcement. It can also help the government be more responsive to its citizens' needs (if it is actually possible for bureaucrats and politicians to be responsive to others' needs). One of the best examples is its use in natural disasters. Over the last generation, satellite images have been used by thousands of officials around the world to assess damage in remote areas or to prevent problems from expanding.

In some cases, satellite images can even prevent problems. For instance, before dams collapse, they usually start leaking more water than usual. Since water and wet ground are readily visible in infrared images, photos will detect a problem dam and, in many cases, help isolate the fault. In fact, a regular program of acquiring images of older dams could be a valuable way to solve problems without spreading the government engineering staff too thin.

But satellite photographs can also be useful in the regular business of government. One of the best examples is in regions experiencing rapid growth. Since maps take years to prepare, most city administrators can't be sure of the changes within the city borders. With satellite photographs, administrators, police, fire, human services, and even campaigning politicians could have up-to-date information. In fact, if the departments need something more accurate than an image, such as a map, orthophotography (Chapter 8 will cover that) offers images with the visual information of a photo and the accuracy of a map.

Satellite images are excellent for determining zoning. Regulators can determine land usage and, by monitoring it regularly, can even see if changes in land use indicate a need to change zoning policies. They can also be used by city planners to locate new city services such as roads and airports.

Much of the information available from satellite images is being put into city databases called Geographical Information Systems (GIS). These databases can look at a part of the town and provide the operator with information on zoning, utilities, ownership, income, dependents, etc. Although they are a powerful tool for city engineers, by combining this information with other databases like credit history, military records, and such, the city bureaucracy has a tool that allows them to look at a house address and learn everything there is to know about the occupants.

Law Enforcement

The marijuana grower was confident. His crops were grown underground and were miles from the nearest person. There wasn't a chance that he would be discovered.

Meanwhile, unseen overhead, a satellite noticed the thermal infrared signature of the ground was different from the surrounding area. That was the first in a chain of events that ended in a ferocious midnight raid by paramilitary police that would have made an aging Gestapo agent proud.

In 1990, bureaucrats of the Metropolitan Water District of Southern California announced they were using LANDSAT images to find people who were watering their lawns too much. Lest the citizenry became too concerned, the official lied and said the satellite could only see something the size of a football field. They implied the average person was safe and the government was only interested in catching the rich people who wasted water. The fact that LANDSAT can see things much smaller than a football field (including well-watered lawns) wasn't mentioned.

It's ironic that satellite surveillance was originally developed to maintain the peace and protect our liberties, but is being used now as a busybody monitoring our every movement from above. Although many of these law enforcement applications can be considered legitimate, there is a growing concern that lawn waterers won't be the last "criminals" arrested by the eye-in-the-sky.

Controversy will always swirl around the civilian use of the military's reconnaissance satellites. Obviously, because they are a national asset, they will not be employed to capture common criminals (like murderers), but in national "crime wars." Ironically, it's these uses that create the greatest possibility for abuse, because wars against crime are always politically inspired campaigns that use all the assets of the country in a "win at all costs" campaign. Unfortunately, this win at all costs mentality leads to the greatest violation of constitutional liberties.

There is no better example of the abuses of a politically inspired crime campaign than the war on drugs. The extremism bred by the war has led the Drug Czar to advocate beheading and severe restrictions on our constitutional rights. It's also led some of our police to resort to torturing suspects in order to elicit information (*Wall Street Journal*, Page 1, January 11, 1991). It's logical, therefore, that spy satellites are thrown into the fray.

Satellites are excellent tools for a campaign against drugs. As I mentioned earlier in this book, each type of plant has a different type of light signature. In addition, most drug crops are grown in neat plots in the wilderness. Therefore, if the spectral information detects a different type of plant, growing in a man-made pattern, in the wilderness, there is a good possibility that the plants are illegal. Thermal infrared images can be used to identify the heat radiated by underground drug farms.

Drug enforcement agents can also find drug plants by using temporal enhancement. By comparing the vegetation from a couple of years, new plots of illegal plants can be identified.

These satellite techniques are already being used in the drug war. Military help in identifying drug crops through reconnaissance photographs has found marijuana crops in Hawaii and California. It has also helped in discovering coca and marijuana crops in South America.

Drug agents have kept the use of satellite intelligence quiet. Usually the information gained from satellites is credited to informants, military reconnaissance aircraft, or spotting planes. However, when you think about it, the idea a pilot can identify a marijuana plant from 500 feet while the aircraft is traveling 200 mph is ludicrous.

A use closely allied to the war on drugs is customs. Today Customs agents use military and civilian satellite information in order to keep the United States' borders closed to smugglers. Keyhole imagery can find airstrips used by smugglers, harbors, warehouses, and can even photograph ongoing operations. Commercial imagery can identify shipping on the high seas, and even detect smuggling trails by sensing the difference between healthy vegetation and that regularly trampled underfoot by smugglers.

A more conventional use of satellite imagery in law enforcement is in patrolling remote areas. Police, who have responsibility for patrolling large areas of wilderness or who are looking for fugitives in a remote area can use up-to-date imagery. Thermal images can help identify campfires, and temporal enhancement can find newly constructed shelters. And, unlike aerial photographs that would alert the fugitives, satellites can gather the information silently.

The ability to identify newly constructed structures is also helpful in finding squatters on federal land. Thanks to soaring property prices and the restrictions of society, more people are trying to start a new life in the wilderness like our pioneer forefathers. With satellites, the Department of Interior can find heat sources that indicate cabins or use temporal enhancement to find changes in the wilderness. This is the only effective way for the government to patrol the millions of acres it owns.

One of the major governmental uses of satellite imagery, especially commercial data, is in the enforcement of environmental laws. Again, thanks to multispectral imagery, subtle changes in the atmosphere, land, vegetation, and water are readily noticed by the analyst. Thanks to its ability to see large areas, the subtle differences that would be ignored on the ground or in a small area can become a part of a larger picture. For instance, a light layer of toxic dust found on the ground hundreds of miles from the source can be traced back to the polluter by studying the pattern of pollution and prevailing winds.

A final law enforcement application is in paramilitary operations. SWAT teams required to storm a remote site may want to avoid using aerial photography either because of the danger to the pilot or the risk of tipping the opposition. In cases like that, commercial multispectral imagery can help identify good approaches, and Keyhole imagery can provide accurate information on the building so even the coarser SPOT imagery and Soviet photographs can provide police with building location and information that may not be available on maps.

Private Investigations

If the government can spy on its citizens, why can't private investigators use the same techniques on the citizen's behalf? Of course, investigators can't use the high resolution Keyhole images, but there is still quite a bit that the LANDSAT, SPOT, and Soviet satellites can provide. It all depends on how well the information is exploited.

Plant security is an obvious use for satellite imagery. In addition to providing much of the same information that conventional satellite photographs would provide, multispectral imagery can detect muddy ground, paths taken by people and vehicles, and other information that will help identify potential security problems.

Ideally, the imagery would be used before the site is built. With satellite imagery and orthophotographs created from the images, the builders can design a facility that avoids security loopholes. Then the security department can regularly purchase imagery to see if any changes have occurred that have an impact on the security. Some of these changes would be new construction by others that may make it easier to penetrate the site (like roads), changes in geography (an impassable swamp dries up), or unexplained occurrences (stress patterns in vegetation that show recent heavy traffic near the site, etc.). By distributing these photos among the roving patrols, the guards could determine areas that require additional attention in regular patrols.

Satellite photographs can also be used by the private investigator in area searches. Like the police, he can use them in searching for lost or hidden people in the wilderness. Although commercial imagery isn't as good as the Keyhole imagery, LANDSAT sensors can detect disturbances in the wilderness, such as large campfires.

Surveillance

Satellite imagery can be useful in surveillance if it is combined with more traditional types of photographic intelligence (for more information on photographic intelligence, read my book *A Practical Guide to Photographic Intelligence*, published by Loompanics). This is especially true in covering large estates or industrial sites where aerial photography is prohibited. It's also beneficial when you need secrecy in a project.

Satellite imagery can help in establishing the surveillance, determining ways to penetrate the site, develop a map of the grounds, and determine important areas. With this information, you can instruct your surveillance team to take ground photographs from the perimeter, which will enhance the satellite information, and give you a better insight into what is happening. If you need photographs from deeper in the restricted area than can be taken with ground photography, you can hire a plane to take photos while staying outside the borders of the area.

Finally, satellite imagery can be used to investigate areas that are too remote, expensive or dangerous to send operatives. Imagine you are asked to provide information on an industrial facility in Beirut, Lebanon. Instead of risking someone in that area, you may be able to answer many questions from satellite images. If you combine that with traditional intelligence sources, you can provide a report just as accurate, with less cost and risk.

7

Earth Resources Applications

Nothing has contributed to the growth of civilian satellite imagery as much as the study of earth resources. Multispectral imagery has helped in the commercial exploration of oil and minerals. But the commercial sector has also contributed much to the science of remote sensing. Geologists and other natural scientists have learned that many things thought to be invisible or hard to detect are visible with multispectral imagery. As a result, our understanding of the earth has grown considerably and military intelligence has acquired new methods of analysis.

Earth resources are also important to satellite imagery because they provide the basic principles and skills that apply to many other applications. Even many law enforcement applications would be worthless without the principles learned in the study of agriculture.

Earth resources applications will continue to grow in the future. Satellite imagery has proven itself to be cheaper than conventional methods in geology and agriculture management. Also, the growing concern about our environment will provide a booming field for satellite analysts. Once the federal government eliminates the draconian laws that punish companies trying to improve environmental quality, it will be easy to see the day when satellite imagery, oriented towards pollution control, may be as common in a corporate boardroom as financial reports.

Geology

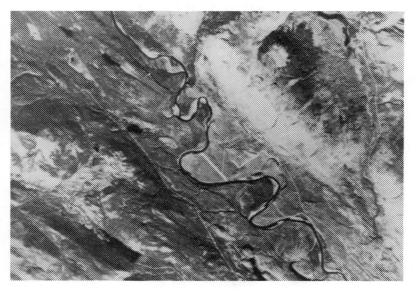

Figure 7-1

Satellite images are excellent for mapping remote areas. This is a Soviet image of a remote region of Canada. Note the dirt airstrip in the center of the photo. An analyst knows the valley is flat because of the wandering river. (Photo courtesy Central Trading Services and The Orthoshop.)

Geologists were accustomed to using aerial photography for finding important geological formations and exploration.

Therefore, it was natural that they would be the first disciples of satellite imagery when it became available from manned space missions in the Sixties. When multispectral imagery came along, it fell neatly in place with the overhead photography they were using.

Geologists routinely use satellite imagery today for structural mapping, mineral and petroleum exploration, and geologic interpretation. By covering large tracts of land quickly, satellite imagery allows commercial geologists to identify promising structures and quickly narrow their search. As a result, satellite exploration is one of the cheapest exploration methods available.

Satellite exploration is also ideal for remote areas where it would be too expensive to support a major geological exploration team on the ground. (See Figure 7-1.) For instance, in New Guinea, Japanese geologists discovered geological structures that led them to believe there was a gold deposit there. When they landed at the site, they discovered their assumptions were right. Their application of satellite photos had saved millions of dollars and years of effort over a traditional exploration project.

What allows geologists to discover minerals? The first clues are spacial characteristics, those that would be obvious from an overhead image. These are major geologic formations like faults, structural traps (that indicate potential oil deposits), and fractures. These are often discovered by the way water drains from the land. Called "creekology" by geologists, the analysis of drainage patterns can provide important clues to the ground structure. For instance, if the creeks have an even drainage pattern reminiscent of a tree and its branches, it usually means the area was originally flat and composed of uniform materials. If the drainage takes sharp turns, it's usually an indication of a fault or fracture. If the drainage is radial, like the spokes of a bicycle, that usually indicates a sink or dome (depending on whether the water goes in or out). Domes are often indicators of petroleum deposits.

Spectral information is also important in geology. Although the minerals look similar to us, their light signature is often radically different. By creating ratio images, geologists can identify different families of minerals. In some cases, the mineral may affect the plants, so by looking at the infrared reflection of the plants, geologists can gain an insight into the geology.

In some cases, multispectral imagery is helping analysts discover spacial features, such as faults. Many faults are old and have virtually disappeared though weathering. By using ratio images, however, scientists have been able to discover the faint traces of ancient faults and fractures that couldn't have been found with conventional methods.

Radar imagery is also important in geological studies. Because it penetrates cloud cover, it's especially useful in exploring tropical areas that are perpetually covered by clouds.

Radar is also useful because it provides sharp images of many fractures and faults, depending on the location and orientation of the satellite. It can also see under ground if the material is dry and has the right characteristics.

One final advantage of satellite imagery in exploration is secrecy. Since mineral exploration is competitive, most companies want to hide their interest in an area. Ground surveys and aerial photography can "tip their hand," but satellite images allow geologists to explore an area secretly. That way, ground exploration isn't used until the last minute and the competition is surprised.

Agriculture

In an earlier chapter, I mentioned that plants reflect infrared light and that it can be seen by satellites. As a result, infrared satellite imagery is becoming more important in agriculture as farmers and government agriculture agents use this information for better crop management.

There are four factors that make satellite imagery ideal for agriculture.

1. Satellite images cover large tracts of ground. This makes such imagery ideal for government agriculture agents to monitor districts or for farmers to obtain a profile of their whole farm. Therefore, large trends can be monitored with ease. For instance, a plant parasite or disease can be tracked as it moves, giving farmers an opportunity to isolate and attack it before it progresses.

2. Each type of plant has its own reflective pattern. Therefore, two different types of crops that appear to be the same from an aerial picture would look drastically different from a multispectral scanner.

3. Plants change their reflective patterns as they mature. In many cases, these patterns have been studied and analysts can tell how far the plant has progressed and if illness or stress has retarded growth. Based on this information, analysts can tell when a crop is ready for harvesting and the potential yield. Farmers can even tell if they will harvest before their neighbors and, therefore, receive higher prices.

4. Satellite images also identify the condition of the ground. An analyst can look over a large area and tell if the fields are too dry or muddy for planting. By carefully monitoring ground condition, farmers can choose their planting time and the right crops.

These factors have been a boon to government agricultural agents. In the past, the large size of the districts and the limited manpower have limited the help these people could provide. Today, with satellite imagery, an agent can scan satellite images and see if any farmers have major problems that he should address. In many cases, what was once the cause for a trip out to a farm can now be taken care of by a phone call, since agents can answer questions at the office based on the information in the images.

Now commercial firms are providing the same information. Farmers can subscribe to a service that monitors their crops, provides them with information about neighbor's yields that may have an impact on prices, and when their crop should be harvested and sold. Considering the speculative nature of commodity prices, an insight into the size of the harvest and possible prices can make the difference between a profit or loss.

Forestry

The principles that allow satellite imagery to be used for agriculture also allow it to help in forestry. However, there are some additional reasons for using satellite imagery to monitor plant health in forestry management.

1. Hundreds of millions of acres of the United States are covered in forests. Since the size is too large for any on-the-ground survey, satellite imagery is the only way to monitor conditions in the whole country.

2. Most forests are remote. Not only do they exist in rugged terrain, they usually have limited roads and trails in them. Satellite imagery allows managers to visit the most remote country with little effort.

3. Satellites can identify the type and maturity of the vegetation in the forest. Commercial lumbering concerns classify profitable lumber stands and government managers note and catalog the different types of vegetation. Since many animals only live in certain types of forest, this gives ecologists an opportunity to protect species before they are destroyed.

4. Satellites can help control forest fires. Thermal imaging can see the hot spots of a fire even though they're covered in smoke. This information can then be passed to firefighters.

More important than limiting fire damage is the new application in preventing fires. The infrared reflectance of plants indicates how dry a plant is. That can provide a warning about potential flash points.

Another application is the identification of different types of vegetation and density. This information can be placed on maps and in a geographical information system. When a fire starts, the computer can predict the future course of the fire, based on the type and density of the vegetation. This gives firefighters an idea of the strength and direction the fire will take. The computer can even give advice on potential strategies for fighting the fire, such as where firebreaks should be placed and sources of water for controlling the fire.

5. Since no one can know everything about a large forest (vegetation, hydrology, ecology, recreational uses, etc.), forestry management is an excellent application for geographical information systems. By using the digital data from a satellite image as the base, forestry managers can develop a database that allows a more efficient use of forests.

Ecology

Ecologists are using satellite imagery to detect pollution. Because it covers large areas, analysts are better able to see pollution that covers hundreds of miles and identify the source of the problem. For instance, a dust cloud may be considered native to an area until a satellite image shows that the area the dust covers is downwind of a major plant.

Satellite imagery can identify land pollution, such as toxic waste dumps, because the spectral response of the toxic materials may be different from the surrounding terrain. In addition, dump sites usually harm the surrounding vegetation so the infrared signature of the local vegetation is much lower than that of the surrounding area.

If the toxic material enters the water table, satellite imagery can follow the poison as plants around the toxic site sicken. If images of previous years are available, analysts can even track the speed of the contamination and predict future effects.

Satellites can also track the pollution of open waters. In 1989, the grounding of the Exxon Valdez in Prince William Sound showed how satellites can follow a spreading oil slick. Although the slick was a composite of oil and water, a principle component analysis could see it in space. The scientists limited themselves to tracking the spill on the water, but there wasn't any reason they couldn't apply the same technology to tracking the oil as it was washed ashore. That could have assisted the clean-up operations.

Water pollution can be tracked from industrial plants because, as it enters the water source, it's warmer than the surrounding water. By using thermal infrared imagery, analysts can see water plumes emitted from industrial facilities such as nuclear power plants. Of course, this plume is more noticeable when the difference between the water source and the effluent is greater. Consequently, thermal infrared imagery is more effective in cold weather than during the summer.

Air pollution is more difficult to find with satellite imagery, but not impossible. One of the most important clues is plant health downwind of the pollution source. As particulate matter settles out of the air, or toxic materials stress the plants, a change should be noticed in the reflectivity in either the plants or the surrounding ground where the particles change the reflective signature.

Another clue to air pollution is the scattering caused by particulate matter in the air. This can either be a tell-tale stream of smoke from a smoke stack or declining resolution in an area. This is especially noticeable in the blue band.

Satellite imagery can also be used for restoring ravaged land, such as strip mines. The image can be stored in a computer, and, based on data from surrounding areas, the image can be manipulated to look as it would after restoration. With a computer, you can view many alternative plans and decide which would fit the surrounding area the best and whether the restoration would cover the damage.

Satellites are a powerful tool for assessing environmental damage. Unfortunately, environmental laws limit its applications and make pollution worse. Most companies are willing to improve the environment and willing to spend money to detect pollution. However, current laws are so strict that if you even think about using satellite imagery to detect your own pollution, you are admitting you are polluting. That information can then be used in court to convict you. As a result, most companies are forced to ignore possible solutions to pollution because to use them is an admission of guilt and can send them to jail.

If the rabid environmental lobby recognizes that cooperation, not confrontation, solves problems, then maybe the laws can change and satellite photos can help make our earth cleaner.

Oceanography

Oceanographic studies have become more important as scientists have come to recognize the ocean's importance in creating weather and providing food. Although the surface may appear to be featureless to the casual observer, satellite imagery can provide many clues to currents and underwater features.

Thermal imagery has been the conventional method for studying currents in the ocean. Most currents have a different temperature than the surrounding water. The Gulf Stream, for instance, is warmer than the surrounding Atlantic and this difference can be seen by a satellite. In fact, most temperature differences in the ocean are directly related to currents.

Temperature differentials aren't as useful for identifying currents in the polar regions, because the temperature differential is less noticeable. However, currents can be noticed, because many currents come from the land and are fresh, sediment laden water. As a result, by studying the thermal information and other visual and infrared bands, many currents can be seen for many miles out into the sea.

Some light penetrates the water and therefore some underwater objects can be seen from space. Red light doesn't penetrate more than 30 feet, so that band is excellent for studying shallow features. Blue and green light can see deeper. Dark blue water usually indicates water deeper than 90 feet. As a result, analysts can distinguish between shallow and deep water to determine if ships can pass.

Radar imaging satellites are ideal for studying the ocean. Unlike conventional images, they can see different waves, so they can study wave patterns and how they relate to currents.

Radar can also notice subtle changes in the level of the water. As a result, in areas where there are strong currents, there is an imperceptible hump over large underwater objects as the water passes over it. This helps oceanographers identify underwater objects. The Navy is also studying this for finding submarines.

Radar can also identify the differing conductivity of ice. As ice grows older, the radar signature changes. This allow scientists to study the flow of ice in the polar icepacks. This is important to protecting shipping near the north and south poles and provides us with a better understanding of the conditions in polar regions.

Summary

Since this is an introductory book, I've given only the barest coverage to many interesting areas. Unfortunately, earth resources is one of them. Many of the most promising applications are found in this chapter and I could spend thousand of pages describing them. Therefore, I just briefly covered the many applications and the principles behind them. While Chapter 12 addresses some interpretation techniques for earth resources, there is still much missing. If you need to know more about these applications, I recommend you look at the books in the Bibliography. These books will give you more information on specific applications and the methods for analyzing the information.

8

Satellite Mapping

It doesn't take a remote sensing expert to look at a satellite image and discover it's perfect for mapping. They can record details from remote parts of the earth that would take surveyors years to find and map, and they can be updated faster than conventional maps. Even in "well mapped" areas, such as the United States, satellite imagery is better than the USGS maps that are often over a generation old and inaccurate.

Of course, one can't just take a satellite photograph and use it as a map. If you did, you might become lost, just as some geologists have had problems finding geological formations from aerial photographs. The reason is that satellite imagery and aerial photographs have distortions that keep them from being as accurate as a map. Some of these distortions are:

1. Atmospheric distortions. If you ever put your arm into water, you noticed that the light makes it appear as if your arm is broken just where it enters the water. Obviously, it isn't fractured; the water has just changed the path of the light in such a way that anything underwater appears in a different place than it really is.

The same thing happens in the atmosphere. At high altitudes or oblique angles, the light waves are distorted as they pass through the air. Consequently, the further light passes through air, the greater the distortion. Therefore, distances and locations of objects in images aren't accurate.

2. The curvature of the earth also distorts images the closer they are to the horizon. The most obvious example is a pair of roads that appear to merge as they reach the horizon. The same thing occurs in space as parallel lines tend to bend towards each other as they head towards the edge of the image.

3. The altitude of objects in the image also affects the scale of the image. Objects that are higher, such as mountains, will appear larger than they should, just as a person closer to a camera will appear larger than those in the background.

4. The satellite optics will also distort the image. This is especially true in wide-angle lenses that are designed to cover large areas. In these images, parallel lines will tend to diverge as they head towards the edge of the image.

The science of correcting photographs is called orthophotography. Orthophotography uses many complex calculations to determine the proper location of objects in images. Although it is generally used in overhead imagery, it's also used in disciplines such as medicine. Doctors can use the same principles to accurately measure the location of parts of the body, based on X-rays or other imaging techniques.

Digital satellite imagery is easier to correct than other photography, because the mathematical corrections can be made by a computer. In fact, some companies that offer satellite imagery can provide you with corrected images when you buy them, so that you don't have to bother with correcting them yourself. Actual photographs, like those offered by the Soviets, require more effort, but it does show how corrected photographs are made.

A good orthophotograph requires stereo photographs (in order to perceive depth and altitude), surveyed ground control points (to determine exact locations), and exact information about the photograph.

The stereo photographs are viewed in a machine that gives the operator a three dimensional representation of the ground. The ground control points that were placed on the ground by a survey team are located in order to provide an idea of the degree of the distortions in the image. The operator can compare the location of the actual ground control points with the apparent points on the image and correct for the distortions with a set of formulas.

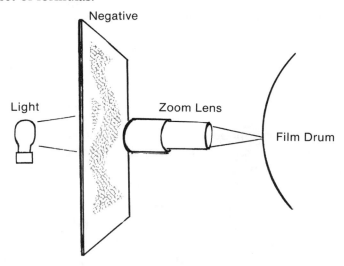

Figure 8-1

Orthophotography, the science of correcting photographs, has been made easier with computers. One process involves beaming light through a negative into a computer controlled lens which transfers the corrected image to film.

The operator then moves the eyepieces across the photograph and determines altitude by moving a marker so it appears to remain in contact with the ground. The information is then stored in a computer.

When the whole image has been analyzed, the data are transferred to a piece of equipment that takes the original negative of the image and applies the corrections to it in order to produce an orthophotograph.

The negative is placed on a glass holder and a narrow beam of light is played through a small part of the negative (usually a slit just a few millimeters long). The light goes through the negative and passes through a zoom lens that automatically makes corrections based on the information provided by the computer and on altitude and distortions (see Figure 8-1). The corrected light beam is then directed towards a drum holding a piece of film. By sweeping back and forth across the original negative, the corrected photograph is produced.

Mapping

Since modern orthophotographs are produced on computers, the information can also be used to create maps. Usually, after the data for ortho products has been collected, the operator reviews the image and records any objects on the photograph.

The location of these objects is then also stored on the computer database. Then a map can be produced just by attaching the computer to a plotter. In some cases, the map is made on a transparent mylar sheet so it can be placed over the orthophotograph in order to provide both a photograph and a map at the same time.

The information used to create a map can also be used to develop a geographical information system (GIS). This computer database allows the user to access information on surface and subsurface features just by entering a location into the computer.

Three-Dimensional Mapping

Thanks to computers, satellite imagery can be turned into a three-dimensional map that can be viewed from any direction on a computer monitor. These are useful in many fields, such as exploration and military applications. For instance, in the Iraqi War, digital images were produced to show bomber pilots how a target would look as the aircraft approached it. The aviators who used it said, "It was just like being there."

The key to producing three-dimensional images is stereo photography. By acquiring two images of the same area, but slightly offset, operators and computers can determine depth, just as two eyes help people determine depth and distance.

With these stereo photographs, the computer can create a digital terrain model (DTM) that shows the height of each spot in the scene. The computer operator can then drape the satellite image over the DTM to provide a realistic view of what the terrain looks like from overhead. Then by rotating the image in the computer with mathematical models, the operator can make the scene appear as it would from any angle viewed by a tank commander or a fighter pilot.

Charleston, South Carolina, as seen by a satellite. The "true color" image shown here is excellent for detecting water depth and manmade objects. The piers of the Charleston Navel Base are obvious, reaching out like fingers in the upper center of the photo. (Photo courtesy Earth Observation Satellite Company.)

This satellite image of Charleston combines information from three bands of light: visible, infrared and near infrared. This provides the analyst with the greatest amount of information. Fort Sumter, nearly invisible in the previous true color image, is the red dot in the bay. Dark brown colors are an indicator of wet soil. (Photo courtesy Earth Observation Satellite Company.)

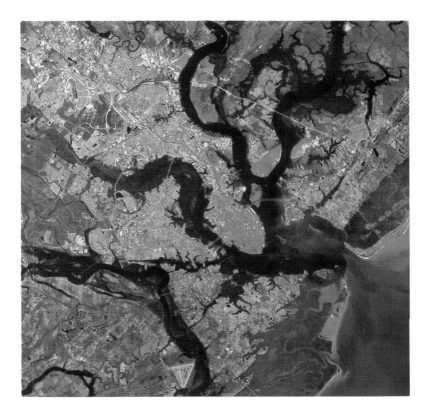

This image of Charleston is made by adding information from the infrared portion of the spectrum to two visible light bands. Vegetation is shown in red. Because plants are strong reflectors of infrared light, it is easier to analyze patterns of vegetation using an infrared image. (Photo courtesy Earth Observation Satellite Company.)

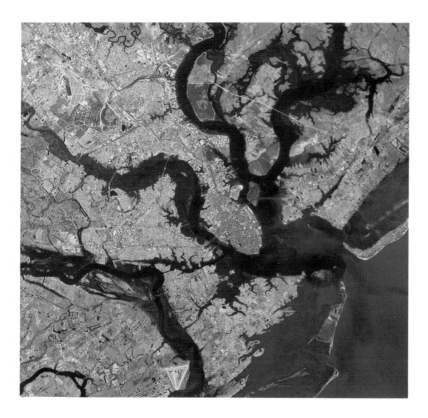

In this satellite image of Charleston, mid-infrared is shown as green (instead of red) so that vegetation will look more natural. Red coloring is an indicator of moisture. Green light is changed to blue. (Photo courtesy Earth Observation Satellite Company.)

9

Engineering Applications

Most highways, bridges, and dams are constructed today with the help of aerial photography. However, with improvements in resolution, satellite imagery can prove to be easier, cheaper, and quicker. Not only can it cover a larger area than the traditional aerial photo, but with multispectral scanning more information can be obtained about ground conditions than before.

Road Construction

Satellite imagery is ideal for road construction, because it can carpet the large areas roads cover without an expensive aerial photography program. The first step consists of a reconnaissance survey, which looks at the general geography and determines several possible routes based on topography, soil, drainage, and the availability of building materials.

After several routes are chosen, engineers compare the several potential routes according to drainage, intersections, right-of-way costs, etc. Although urban roads need more detail than a commercial satellite image provides today, rural routes could be planned with satellite photographs. This process will inevitably give engineers just a few possible routes.

The final choice of route is made by producing orthophotographs (with topographic contours) of the proposed routes and making a cost analysis based on distances, grading, and necessary construction. The information gained in this manner will provide the final basis for selecting the best route.

Bridge Construction

Often the largest cost of any road project is constructing the bridges. Therefore, a poorly chosen bridge location can easily cause construction costs to skyrocket.

The major difference between bridge and road construction is water. The depth of the water, as well as the condition of the ground on both sides of the proposed bridge, affects the cost. With multispectral imagery, analysts can often determine the depth of the water and the type of ground that the structure will have to be built on. Although a ground survey will be required, satellite imagery can help narrow the prospects quickly and with less cost.

Dams and Reservoirs

Hydroelectric power is based on the topography of the region. The most effective sites have high banks (common in mountainous regions) which hold water, a steep grade where water can gain energy as it falls downhill, and sufficient rain. Satellite imagery can help determine potential sites in a large area. Stereo photographs can help the analyst estimate if the ground has the right characteristics, while multispectral imagery can determine if the area has sufficient water.

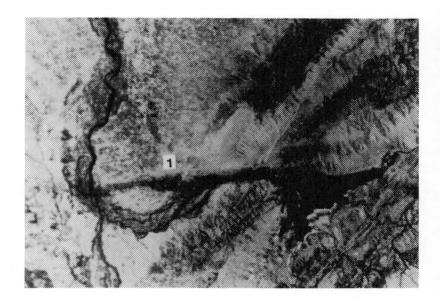

Figure 9-1

This infrared image from India shows leakage from a dam. The dark zone (1) extending from the reservoir indicates wet ground.

Studying the feasibility of reservoirs either requires an extensive aerial photography campaign or satellite imagery because the engineer must not only be aware of the hydrology of the area, but must also be sure of the size of the watershed the reservoir is affecting. Infrared imagery can help identify small streams, water content of the ground, and the potential risk of sedimentation in the reservoir.

Satellite imagery can also find leaking and damaged dams. Since infrared images can detect wet dirt, a satellite image can detect leaks in dams that may be the precursor to a major break. (See Figure 9-1.)

Summary

Satellite photographs are just becoming important to engineering. Unfortunately, the current restrictions on resolution by governments have limited its applications, because many uses need better resolution than the 30 to 5 meters offered by commercial satellites. However, if engineers can obtain images with the resolution of the Keyhole spacecraft, the number of applications will mushroom in the future.

10

Entertainment
and
Other Applications

Satellite imagery is still in its infancy, so many applications have yet to be discovered. Here are a few other uses.

Media

On Saturday, April 26, 1986, the number 4 nuclear reactor at Chernobyl went critical and exploded with the power of 1000 pounds of TNT, the equivalent of a small tactical nuclear warhead. That and other secondary explosions tossed the lid off the reactor and blew the walls out. In the following days, the graphite core continued to burn while spewing radioactive material out into the atmosphere. Days later, the US learned of the accident because air samples showed abnormal amounts of radioactivity and communications intelligence satellites indicated abnormal activity around Kiev. The intelligence community then directed the lone KH-11 to take photographs of the damaged reactor.

What the government saw was men playing soccer at the plant, the graphite core still on fire, and Soviet MI-8 helicopters dousing the reactor with sand and lead pellets. Unfortunately, the intelligence community wasn't about to share this Keyhole intelligence with the rest of the world.

The population finally saw the destruction thanks to the LANDSAT and SPOT satellites. This was the media's first serious application of satellites in news reporting and the results were worthwhile. The images showed the damaged building, the burning core, and an unused cooling pond. For the first time, the citizen had a chance to see what the intelligence community had been looking at for a quarter of a century.

Chernobyl started the ball rolling. Now satellite images are regularly seen in newspapers and on network news. They are ideal for wars where the opponents refuse to provide accurate news coverage. As a result, they were used extensively by news agencies in the Iran/Iraq war. These photos showed Silkworm missile deployments in the Persian Gulf and tanks on the front line. They also showed Iraqi positions in Kuwait in the recent conflict with the US.

Satellites have given Americans a better understanding of strategic issues, as SPOT has regularly covered Soviet military and nuclear sites such as the nuclear test facilities at Semipalatinsk or launch facilities at Tyuratum. They have even become a part of the debate about arms limitations agreements by showing Americans what can be verified by national technical means.

Commercial satellites also give the public a chance to learn about events that were once known only to the intelligence communities. For instance, in 1988 a story in the *Chicago Tribune* published SPOT images that indicated an accident at a Soviet Nuclear complex in 1957.

But most surprising is that commercial imagery can even correct intelligence analysis. In 1990, the White House reported a Libyan chemical warfare plant had been destroyed by fire. On March 18th, the SPOT satellite photographed an untouched factory, leading analysts to believe the fire was at a building a kilometer away. The next week the US government backed away and said their initial assessment of the damage was wrong.

Investing

What a satellite photograph can tell a farmer about a crop, it can tell an investor. Therefore, commodity research firms can use satellite information of critical growing areas to see what the potential yield will be and if serious weather conditions will ruin the crops. This information is also valuable for industries like food processors, who want to purchase supplies while prices are low.

Satellite imagery can also help investors acquire information about closed societies. For instance, platinum investors are always concerned about Soviet platinum production. With satellite imagery, they can track production at the mines by counting ore cars, how much earth is moved, and smoke stack emissions. It's the next best thing to inside information.

Art

Color satellite imagery can be striking. As a result, posters of local areas, as seen from a satellite, are becoming popular items in poster shops. Within a decade every major city in the US will probably have a satellite poster available for sale.

Archeology

Overhead photography has become popular in finding evidence of ancient cities and burial mounds. Now, with the help of multispectral scanning, archaeologists can find evidence of ancient sites by detecting the different reflective signature of the artifacts and the surrounding area.

Radar imagery can help archaeologists look underground. In the Middle East, scientists have found irrigation ditches buried centuries ago by the blowing sands.

Writing

A good writer usually visits the setting of his book. That's a good idea, unless you are writing a spy thriller set in a top secret military facility. Of course, you can fake it, but the results are never as satisfying, and one of your readers may have visited the area.

If you can't visit the locality, why not buy a satellite image of the area? For less than the cost of a plane ticket, you can visit any place in the world via satellite imagery. If you use a magnifying glass you can see all the buildings your characters will visit and gain a familiarity with the place that will make your book sparkle.

11

Avoiding
Satellite Detection

For every person who wants to see something with a satellite, there's probably someone who wants to avoid detection. Some are civil libertarians, who don't like the idea of Big Brother spying on them. However, the most practical application of satellite deception is in the military.

Ironically, the secrecy we cloak our reconnaissance satellites with hinders our own armed forces in hiding from the opposition. While almost everyone knows about spy satellites, they have a imperfect idea about avoiding their attention. The soldiers, who are expected to fight the next war, have little idea about how to hide from satellite detection, and the engineers, who design our equipment, still think a dab of camouflage paint will hide them. These assumptions are dangerous.

There are several ways someone can lessen the possibility of satellite detection. In the hope of protecting American troops, here are some ideas for avoiding unwanted attention.

Avoid Attention

While the intelligence community and their contractors have made amazing strides in technical collection methods, our ability to analyze and process the information is limited. We have satellites that can send back hundreds of thousands of images, but the bottleneck occurs in trying to interpret them, because much of the analysis still rests on the shoulders of a trained interpreter.

Agencies like the CIA have developed software that allows computers to automatically spot changes in images with temporal enhancement techniques. This takes some of the load from the analysts, because it can sort through lower priority images. However, these systems don't have the intelligence of a person, so many things still can be missed. Therefore, important targets are still given to humans because computers can be easily fooled by changing shadows or the time of year.

Efforts have also been directed at improving image recognition by computer. In the 1980s, the intelligence community used two parallel processing computers that could count ships and aircraft (even identifying types) and warn analysts if there was a dramatic change. It doesn't replace the analyst so much as handle some mundane tasks such as counting equipment.

There is no doubt that both Soviet and American photographic interpreters have their hands full analyzing known targets. Automated interpretation is still in its infancy and is directed towards known targets. That means the best way to avoid attention is to stay away from targets that receive attention. For instance, if the Soviets build a new facility next to a nuclear missile site, there's a greater chance it will be noticed than if it was built out in the frozen tundra of Siberia. The only reason U-2 pilots discovered the Russian rocket site of Tyuratam was that they discovered railroad tracks leading nowhere.

By locating potential targets in non-threatening areas, you can limit the risk the enemy will photograph the site and the risk it will be seen by an analyst if it is photographed.

Deception

The Soviets are masters of deception. Consequently, they have devoted quite a bit of effort to deceiving the Keyhole satellites. According to Soviet defector Viktor Suvorov (a pseudonym), a computer that tracks the orbits of all spy satellites has been installed in the Central Command of the Chief Directorate of Strategic Deception. They inform military units when to hide secret assets and when they can be left outside.

The Soviets have used other means of deception. One of the most common is with the paint can and brush. In the 1960s, ICBM bases were painted in order to camouflage the missiles. Apparently this method has been abandoned.

Dummy complexes and roads have also been used by the USSR with some success. Generally, these are surface-to-air missile sites designed to confuse the US military when it identifies potential targets.

The Soviets also cover targets with tarpaulins. Although this doesn't hide the location of the target, it does confuse the status. For instance, the Soviets hid their submarines in the early 1970s in order to confuse US intelligence about their readiness. This deception was so disruptive that US/Soviet agreements later banned this behavior in the case of strategic arms.

The Soviets have also tried to deceive satellites with dummy equipment. In the early 1970s, a severe storm in the Northern

Pacific hit a Soviet naval base. Keyhole photos taken after the storm showed broken and bent dummy submarines tossed about by the winds and waves.

A better way for hiding Soviet submarines is by building tunnels in cliffs by the ocean. These can hide the largest submarines, yet are invisible to US satellites.

Other Soviet deception methods are:

1. Making one piece of equipment look like another.

2. Moving equipment inside when satellites pass overhead.

3. Digging false impact craters at test facilities in order to deceive the US about missile accuracy.

4. Painting patterns that look like streets and houses on runways.

The Soviets aren't the only ones to practice deception. The Israelis carefully monitored aircraft activity at their base in Eilat so satellites couldn't detect any difference in numbers before Israel attacked the Iraqi nuclear reactor at Osirak.

Although these methods have had limited success in the past, they are based on traditional deception practiced for years against traditional cameras. Unfortunately, with new satellites, these traditional methods will not be as effective. Infrared detectors can tell the difference between vegetation and camouflage, thermal infrared detectors can see the difference in temperature between a real and dummy aircraft, modern satellites can vary their orbit to upset schedules, and multispectral imagery can see the most clever camouflage. As a result, new methods are required if the military hopes to hide from the reconnaissance satellites in the future.

First, determine the type of satellite that may be looking for you. Each has weaknesses that can be exploited. For instance, someone trying to hide from a Keyhole satellite can use deception methods that would not fool the LANDSAT multispectral scanner. On the other hand, a critical missile complex must expect to be viewed by all possible methods. The following list specifies the basic types of deception that can be used against each type of satellite.

Modern Military Satellites — panchromatic deception, thermal imaging deception.

Military Satellites With Film Cameras — photographic deception.

Radar Satellites — radar deception.

Multispectral Satellites — Multispectral deception, thermal imaging deception (for LANDSAT).

General Deception Techniques

There are several satellite deception methods that apply to any type of image.

Don't Be Obvious

Try to blend into the background. Tanks shouldn't be parked in a field and aircraft shouldn't be out in the open. If possible, hide in a confusing background. For instance, tanks would be harder to notice in a village with small buildings, because the tanks would blend in with their surroundings.

Avoid Manmade Patterns

Nothing catches the eye of a photo interpreter quicker than a manmade pattern such as a square, triangle, star, etc. Try to break up the regular patterns with camouflage or by moving some equipment. If you are using camouflage netting, avoid square pieces and don't place them in a regular pattern.

Use Natural and Confusing Patterns

Objects can be better hidden if they follow natural patterns. Cliffs often offer some protection from overhead photography if the equipment is kept close to the walls. Streams usually have different types of vegetation close to their banks, so equipment hidden along the banks would be harder to identify. Obviously, hiding something in a forest is better than in the open.

Camouflage the Surrounding Area

By camouflaging parts of the surrounding area, you can confuse the interpreter about the location and number of targets. If enough camouflage is used and it has a high infrared signature, it may even look like another variety of vegetation.

Beware of Resolution Limits

Satellites can see things smaller than their resolution if the contrast is high or if patterns around the area give an idea of its use. For instance, a signal mirror could easily be seen from space even though it's only a couple of inches in diameter. Patterns can also give away location; for example, a star pattern suggests a Soviet surface-to-air site or a diamond indicates a baseball field.

If an interpreter has an idea of a facility's use, he can easily identify and count objects too small to be identified by the image. For instance, an interpreter can use the coarse resolution of a LANDSAT image (30 meters) to count aircraft on the apron of an airport even though the aircraft are less than 100 feet in length because the aircraft affect the reflective pattern and leave telltale smudges.

Panchromatic Deception

Black and white images from satellites are usually produced by CCDs. Although they offer the best resolution, they are limited to the visible bands of light and near infrared. They can be masked to see only certain bands of light, such as green, red, etc., but that limits the amount of energy that enters the sensor and therefore decreases the sensitivity. Therefore, black and white images are more common, and objects are differentiated by their total reflectivity, not their color. This causes their biggest weakness.

Decoys Work

CCDs aren't as sensitive to different reflective patterns, so decoys can fool the satellite. These are used extensively by both the Soviets and US, and inventories exist of decoys that are either inflated or are made of lightweight panels. Since reconnaissance satellites often take stereo images, three-dimensional decoys are better than flat ones that just lay on the ground.

Color Patterns Aren't as Effective

A camouflage pattern that depends on different colors to confuse, instead of different tones, will be less effective in a B&W picture.

On the positive side, colors don't mean as much, so copying the exact tint of a tank camouflage isn't as important when you are making a decoy.

CCDs Can't See Through Clouds

The light that CCDs detect is effectively blocked by cloud cover, therefore, overcast days are ideal for troop movements.

CCDs Can See in Low Light Situations

That's because they are more efficient than film, and computers can enhance low light images. Therefore, they can detect objects at dawn and sunset with little difficulty. They can also see in shadows, with the proper computer enhancement.

Thermal Image Deception

Unlike infrared, thermal infrared sees the heat emitted from objects. This allows them to separate hot tanks from cold dummies and even see through some cloud cover or during the night. The Gallium Arsenide detectors are larger than CCDs, so the resolution isn't as fine.

Summer Degrades Thermal Imagers

As in normal photography, much depends on contrast. In the winter, a hot object stands out from the cold ground. During the summer, however, the warm ground confuses the image and lowers contrast. Analysts won't be able to gather as much information during the summer as they can during the winter.

Cloud Cover Can Degrade Thermal Imaging

Although thermal imagers can see through some clouds, the water and particles scatter the infrared energy and smear the resulting image. This is especially true in a summer rainstorm, where the background heat confuses the sensors; the rain cools hot objects, and the cloud cover smears the image.

Nights Are Dangerous

Not only can thermal sensors see in the night, the colder background makes the contrast higher. Obviously, winter nights are more dangerous than summer nights.

Give Dummies Thermal Signatures

Military dummies often have heat generators to simulate engines. This gives it the same look to a thermal imager as a real piece of equipment.

Don't Give Benchmark Temperatures

If an analyst knows the temperature of one of the objects on the ground, he can judge the temperatures of all the other objects. For instance, a campfire near some dummy tanks can give an analyst a clue to the temperatures on the ground. Then by comparing that known temperature with that of the "hot" tanks, he can see if the heat from the engine compartments is from an engine or a heat generator.

Thermal Imagers Can See Underground

The heat from an underground bunker can be seen as it heats the ground above it. The temperature of underground facilities must be about the temperature of the surrounding ground. Extra heat must be dissipated.

Underground Heat Can Be Dissipated by Mixing with Cold Air

In order to reduce thermal signatures on aircraft and ships, they mix the hot exhaust gases with colder air from the atmosphere. By adding cold air to hot exhaust air before it goes out, the final air temperature isn't much different from the ambient temperature.

Insulate

The same principles that pertain to insulating your house for winter apply to reducing the thermal signature of your equipment. Dead air space and fiberglass can cut the thermal signature significantly.

Cover Hot Objects

Heavy vegetation can hide a thermal signature. If you don't have a tropical rain forest available, the thermal blankets found in survival kits can reflect heat. Hang one above the object (avoid contact so the dead air space acts as an insulator) and place the camouflage tarpaulin above it.

Multispectral Deception

As we mentioned in earlier chapters, multispectral scanners can see more than we can possibly imagine. Therefore, we can't effectively use inexpensive or lightweight dummies because even the reflective pattern from the material will probably be different. However, these sensors have coarser resolution, so there is an opportunity to deceive them.

Use Natural Materials

Manmade materials, including camouflage, don't have the signature of natural materials. Structures made of natural material will blend in easier.

If the material is cut, the dying plant will lose its infrared reflection and stand out to the sensor. The best way to avoid this is to keep covering the structures with freshly cut, leafy material every day. The old material should be spread around in the forests and fields to lower the vegetation's infrared reflection and avoid attracting attention to a large dump. Cut vegetation can also be used longer if it's kept moist.

Clouds Hide Objects from Multispectral Sensors

Visual and infrared light can't penetrate clouds. Nor can it penetrate night, because it depends on the sun for light.

Hide in Confusing Backgrounds

Since every type of plant has a different type of reflection, you can confuse interpreters by hiding in a forest with a variety of types of vegetation. An unusual reflective signature will not stand out in a mixed forest as much as in a forest with a predominant plant type, say, maples.

Stay Small

Small structures made with natural materials will be more likely to avoid detection from the coarse sensors of multispectral sensors.

Cover Manmade Objects With Natural Materials

This won't guarantee that they won't be detected, but it will make the job harder, especially if the object is small.

Photographic Deception

Although superseded by electronic imagery, photographic satellites will still be used by the USSR and smaller countries that launch their first crude reconnaissance satellites. Here's how they can be deceived:

Keep Moving

Film has to be brought down and processed before it can be interpreted. This can take days or even weeks. Obviously, the information will be worthless if your unit has moved.

Operate Under Clouds

The energy that film records is blocked by clouds and night. Operate under these conditions.

Decoys Work

Since film isn't as sensitive to many parts of the electromagnetic spectrum, most decoys work. The main exception to this is camouflage. The infrared detected by film can tell the difference between vegetation and traditional camouflage.

Work Under Low Light

Film isn't as sensitive as CCDs, so low light conditions, shadows, and low contrast confuse film more than electronic images.

Radar

The technology for evading radar imaging satellites is much like that employed in stealth aircraft. Review some books on stealth technology for more ideas on evading attention.

Eliminate or Hide Reflecting Surfaces

A large reflecting surface, such as a tank deck, is a strong radar reflector. These should be covered with a thick layer of absorbing materials like vegetation (a log structure), or dirt (the dirt should be as moist as the surrounding ground).

The same goes for corners, because 90 degree corners act like the reflector of a flashlight and send a strong signal back to the receiver. In fact, if you are designing military equipment, all surfaces should be rounded and corners eliminated when possible, because radar satellites are used to find military forces under clouds.

Hide in Strong Reflectors

Certain geological features like faults, cliffs, and fractures are strong radar reflectors because radar bounces right back to the receiver. By hiding equipment in these large reflectors, the returning signal is so strong that it washes out the image of the equipment.

Passive Radar

Passive radar is hard to detect and hard to hide from. Since advances in this field are cloaked in secrecy, I have to make educated guesses as to its characteristics.

Passive radar is closer in operation to the thermal imager than the traditional radar, because the strength of the signal depends on the temperature of the object instead of its reflectivity. The hotter the object, the more obvious it is. Consequently, if the temperature of the object is close to that of the surrounding area, the radar signal will be about the same.

Of course, sophisticated passive radar won't just depend on a signal. Computers will see if the object is moving in relation to the background, which would indicate it is manmade rather than natural. By employing synthetic aperture passive radar, resolution would be better and distances could be determined.

Deceiving passive radar (also called passive microwave) would depend on keeping the target's temperature close to that of the background. Decoys can also be deployed that are hot and move. If the targets are dispersed and small, that should make the interpreter's task harder.

Summary

Any military man will tell you intelligence about the opponent is critical. At the same time, the technology required to orbit a satellite is becoming available to more countries. It makes sense, therefore, that even if we never battle the Soviets, we will inevitably meet a foe with reconnaissance satellites.

The problem with avoiding satellites is that a method for evading attention from one will probably attract attention from another. For instance, a grid of lights above a target could perfectly match the reflective signature of the surrounding area and become invisible to a multispectral satellite. However, it would be painfully obvious to a high resolution panchromatic CCD satellite when viewed from an angle. Given that problem, the types of deception I mentioned were simple and didn't increase the attention from other systems.

Of course, the best method for avoiding attention is to be where they aren't looking. A well placed unit, with the barest cover, will be better hidden than a poorly placed one with all the camouflage in the world.

Part III

Personal Access
to
Satellite Technology

12

Buying
Satellite Services

In the first part of this book we discussed how satellites work and how they produce imagery. In the second part, we discussed how the images can be applied to many tasks. In the third part we will move from the theoretical to the practical and talk about how you can actually acquire these images, what equipment you need, and how to begin using them yourself.

Acquiring Satellite Images

Buying satellite imagery is just as simple as ordering from a mail order catalog. If you know the latitude and longitude of the target and have arranged a way to pay for it, you can telephone and actually order it on the phone. If they have it in their film library, you can have your images in a few days. If you need a new acquisition, you will have to wait until the satellite is overhead again.

I will pass over the details of ordering because they are different for each company and that information is available from them. You can find out more by calling or writing the companies listed in Chapter 14. However, before you order you will need to know the location of the target and what type of product you want.

The products range from photographic prints of the image to magnetic tapes of geographically corrected data. They also range from about $100 to over $5,000. As usual, the more you spend, the more useful it is.

Prints

The cheapest products are usually paper prints, not much different from the enlargements you would receive from a film processor. Although they don't allow you to do the sophisticated enhancement mentioned in earlier chapters, they are very inexpensive and only require a magnifying glass to use. In some cases, you can custom order prints that show certain spectral responses and even some enhancements. These are ideal for anyone who needs basic information about a target and doesn't have sophisticated equipment.

Transparencies

The next most expensive product is a transparency (the same thing as a large slide) or a negative. It allows the interpreter to make prints and is convenient for showing to groups with an overhead projector. Obviously, it requires an overhead projector or light table to use. As with prints, you can usually order different bands of light and some basic enhancement. This product is excellent for people who need to produce prints for distribution.

Stereograms

These are a pair of images that show the same object from slightly different positions in order to give the interpreter a sense of depth when viewing them with the right equipment. They are either available as prints or transparencies (depending on the type of equipment you have). In order to view them you need a stereoscope (pocket models cost about $20). This product is excellent for people who need to know the elevation of the terrain or who want to make a better analysis of the target.

Until now we've dealt with photographic products. They are cheap to buy and easy to interpret. Now we take a quantum leap into the high-cost world of computers and sophisticated enhancement.

Magnetic Tape

This is the digitized version of the images. The tape has each pixel of the image and the light responses from each band. With the tape you can do the most sophisticated analysis of the target you need.

In order to use the tape, you need a suite of expensive computer support. I won't go into the specific types of equipment available, because computer technology is changing so fast that, by the time this goes to print, the computers I mention may be obsolete. However, the satellite companies can direct you towards the right equipment and software for your needs.

You will need a computer and monitor with graphic capability and a tape drive. Then you will want to buy some software that manipulates the data in the manner you want. In some cases, you can rent the equipment and software, if you only need it for a short time.

If you have a sophisticated task, you might want to hire an expert interpreter. In that case, you might want to contact the American Society for Photogrammetry and Remote Sensing in Bethesda, MD (the address is in Chapter 14). They can assist you in your search.

You will also need some texts, if you want to delve more deeply into the subject. Some basic texts are found in the Bibliography, but one special reference is the *Multispectral Users Guide,* produced by Autometric and 3M. It discusses the best enhancement methods and how to apply them to analysis. The 200-plus photographs are all first generation images and the information and the pictures make it worth the $975 price.

If you decide to apply sophisticated computer analysis to satellite imagery, be sure to bring your wallet. If you shop around for used equipment, you might be able to start for less than a few thousand dollars. However, you will be unable to fully exploit your satellite information.

Value Added Services

If the price of establishing your own satellite imagery interpretation department scared you, don't worry. Several companies have the equipment and experts to manipulate and interpret the data for you. These are usually called value added services and some of companies that provide them are found in Chapter 14. A more complete list can be acquired from the satellite companies.

A value added company can save you a considerable amount of money. Obviously, they can cut your costs because they already have the equipment and personnel. They know what you are looking for and can often find it faster than you.

These companies also have libraries with satellite data. If your target is found in their library, they usually let you use the data free of charge. If not, you will have to buy it first. If they have the data, you only have to pay the cost for using their services. In 1991, one company charged $75 an hour; not much more than the price of an auto mechanic. If they have the data you need and you use them for half a day, you can walk away with the analysis you need for as little as $300. That's like having sophisticated enhancement and analysis for the cost of a photograph.

Unless you have an ongoing need for satellite imagery, the best solution for using digital satellite imagery is to hire a value added company. Their prices are reasonable and the equipment and personnel they offer are much better than what you can buy for much more.

Summary

Satellite imagery prices range from hundreds to thousands of dollars. As with most things in life, the more you spend the more you get. A couple of hundred dollars will give you good spacial information and can be analyzed with a magnifying glass. A search for mineral deposits can cost thousands of dollars if you include the cost of data, equipment, software, and personnel. If your need is limited, it makes sense to hire a firm that has the equipment and personnel. The choice is yours.

13

Interpreting
Satellite Images

Commercial satellite imagery allows the analyst to choose between several types of images with different resolution and band width. In order to clarify the choices, here's a list of the commercial satellites, the bands they offer, and their resolution.

KFA 1000 (Soviet)
(Resolution 5 meters)

Green/Red Band. .56 to .67 microns. This one band allows the analyst to see most natural and manmade objects.

Infrared Band. .76 to .81 microns. Because of the high infrared reflection of plants, this band is best for studying vegetation.

KATE 200 (Soviet)
(Resolution 15-30 meters)

Green Band. .5 to .6 microns. Deep water, atmosphere, and vegetation analysis.

Red Band. .6 to .7 microns. Studying manmade objects, shallow water, vegetation, and soil. Since red light doesn't scatter as much, this is the best visible band for viewing.

Infrared Band. .7 to .9 microns. Studying vegetation.

LANDSAT
(Resolution 30 meters)

Band 1. Blue light, .45 to .52 microns. Atmospheric and deep water studies (up to 150 feet deep in clear water).

Band 2. Green light, .52 to .6 microns. Deep water (up to 90 feet in clear water) and vegetation studies. Similar results to band 1.

Band 3. Red light, .6 to .69 microns. Excellent for studying manmade objects, shallow water (less than 30 feet), vegetation, and soil.

Band 4. Near infrared, .76 to .9 microns. Best band for vegetation studies.

Band 5. Mid infrared, 1.55 to 1.75 microns. Plant and soil moisture studies. This band can see some fires.

Band 6. Thermal infrared, 10.4 to 12.5 microns. Resolution is 120 meters. Readings are from emitted, not reflected energy. Excellent for night studies, thermal differences in water, forest fires, and geological structures.

Band 7. Mid Infrared, 2.08 to 2.35 microns. Excellent for studying soil, geological features, clays, silicates, moisture, and fires.

MK-4 (Soviet)
(Resolution 5-8 meters)

Blue/Green Band. .46 to .585 microns. Atmospheric and deep water studies.

Green Band. .515 to .565 microns. Atmospheric, deep water, and vegetation studies.

Red Band. .635 to .69 microns. For studying manmade objects, shallow water, vegetation, and soil.

Near Infrared Band. .81 to .9 microns. Best band for vegetation studies.

Red/Infrared Band. .58 to .8 microns. For studying manmade objects, vegetation, and soil.

Panchromatic Band. All visible light, .4 to .7 microns. Covers most natural and manmade objects.

SPOT
(Resolution 10 or 20 meters)

Panchromatic Band. Red and green light, .5 to .73 microns. Resolution is 10 meters. Highest digital resolution. Covers most natural and manmade objects. Can be merged with other SPOT and LANDSAT data to improve resolution.

Green Band. .5 to .59 microns. Deep water, atmosphere, and vegetation studies. 20 meter resolution.

Red Band. .61 to .68 microns. For studies of manmade objects, shallow water, vegetation, and soil. Resolution is 20 meters.

Near Infrared Band. .79 to .89 microns. Best band for vegetation studies. Resolution is 20 meters.

Multicolor Images

The commercial satellites offer a total of 22 bands of information. Even though the Soviet images are from film, they can be digitized and used like those from LANDSAT and SPOT. When you combine them into color composites, you can use three bands. That means you have 441 different combinations of data. Then you have 6 different color combinations with each set of three bands (represented by red, green, and blue). That means there are 2,646 different image possibilities from the same scene. That doesn't even take into account the infinite possibilities of enhancement methods. Obviously, even experts can be confused about what method of analyzing data is best.

Fortunately, there are only a few combinations that provide most of the information. The rest of the other enhancement methods and band combinations are useful only in unusual circumstances.

The most popular combination is the true-color image. In it, the green band is green on the image, the blue is blue, and red is red. The result is what a person would expect to see from overhead. It's useful for studying water and manmade objects and, since it's what we are conditioned to see, analyzing it is easier for the beginner.

Another popular color combination is the traditional infrared image, where one of the primary colors is eliminated and infrared is substituted. For instance, green, red and infrared can be displayed in green, red, and blue respectively. In a picture like this, strong infrared reflectors like vegetation would be a strong blue. This has been a popular choice for detecting vegetation and camouflage.

There is a way to logically narrow down the other 2,644 choices — eliminate redundant information. For instance, the green band from SPOT and LANDSAT, although different, obviously display virtually the same information. Thus, we can narrow the 22 bands into 4 groups where the information in each group is virtually the same. They are:

.4 to .7 microns. This is visible light. It's the only group that can see under water and tends to scatter more (less in the red).

.75 to .9 microns. This is the near infrared band. Since vegetation is an excellent reflector in this band, it is the best for studying vegetation.

1.5 to 2.35. This is the middle infrared band. It can detect moisture content and can detect hot objects like fires.

10.4 to 12.5. This is the far infrared or thermal infrared. This shows emitted energy instead of reflected energy. It's good for night studies, detecting water currents, and geological structures.

We now have four groups. Since we can only display three colors, we will eliminate the thermal band (since the information from it is of limited use and the resolution is worse). That leaves three families of energy, one for each primary color. If you make a color composite image using data from each of the three groups, you will probably have most of the information available in the image.

The choice of color combinations is personal, but consistency makes interpretation easier and certain colors, such as red, stand out, making some information more noticeable.

One of the choices you have to make is what color infrared should be. Traditionally infrared has been displayed as red since infrared is closer to red and is often associated with heat. However, since plants reflect infrared, these images showed red vegetation, which made some analysts uncomfortable. Therefore, they made the color for infrared green. The choice is up to you.

In this case, we will assign green to the band where vegetation reflects the most light, the near infrared (.75 to .9 microns). We will assign the other infrared band to the traditional red (1.5 to 2.35 microns, the mid infrared group). That leaves visible light in the blue band (.4 to .7 microns).

We now have a useful tool for making color composites; blue is visible light, green is near infrared light, and red is middle infrared. Now, by using the information from earlier in the chapter that shows what each band displays best, we can create a color image that meets our needs.

Let's say we needed a satellite image of a possible insertion point for a covert military operation. We need to see where the shallow water is, so the boats won't run aground. We want to know where the vegetation is, so we can stay undetected, and we want to know the ground moisture, so we won't be hindered by muddy ground. The keys are:

1. Shallow water. That means we want the red band (.6 to .7 microns) because it shows submerged objects in less than 30 feet of water. This will be displayed in blue. Red is also good at showing manmade objects, so it will indicate any buildings.

2. Vegetation. We want the middle infrared band (.75 to .9 microns) because vegetation is a strong reflector in middle infrared. That will be displayed in green.

3. Muddy ground. We will use LANDSAT band 5 (1.55 to 1.75 microns) because it indicates moisture in vegetation and the soil. Band 5 will also detect large fires in villages.

We now have one satellite image that will contain all the information we need for the mission. We can also look at other photos, such as thermal images, to look for more signs of habitation, but this one picture will have most of the data we need for the mission.

Along with blending light bands into color composites, the analyst can also enhance the images with some methods we discussed earlier in the book. Although the complex enhancement methods can help, simple methods such as edge and stretch enhancement are very effective and usually are all the interpreter needs. With these few tools, you can do the following sophisticated interpretation.

Airfields

Airports are important for either military or urban studies. Among other things, the interpreter wants to discover if the airfield is military or civilian, if the field handled bombers or fighters, or if the field is a small dirt runway for local traffic or military dispersal. One of the best color composites consists of blue light, near infrared, and LANDSAT band 7.

Civilian Airports

Civilian airports are more closely tied into the community than military airfields. Major roads lead to the facility, major parking is available (in the developed countries), and large terminals are available for the passengers. The aprons are usually smaller than with military fields, taxiways are shorter, and there are no embankments to protect from bomb damage.

Fighter Airfields

Fighter bases have protected hangers, embankments, and cement aprons that allow the planes to disperse. Taxiways are larger than with commercial fields.

Bomber Bases

Cement aprons are larger. Taxiways are longer. Isolated ammunition storage facilities are usually located near by.

Dirt Fields

These have lower reflection because they are made with dirt. There are usually few buildings.

Cities

Cities are easy to detect because roads are excellent reflectors. The red band is usually the best for viewing urban areas.

American Cities

Cities in the Americas are usually spread out and the roads provide a checkerboard pattern with suburbs surrounding the urban area. Businesses and industrial areas are usually clumped into zones throughout the city. There is some sign of city planning, so there are large roads and airports near the major thoroughfares.

Old Asian Cities

The center of the town is dense and hard to see with coarse resolution. Road patterns are uneven and resemble a maze. Many walled compounds are also evident. Modern facilities like airports are on the outskirts. No central planning or major roads are in evidence.

Modern Eastern European and Third World Cities

There are large apartment complexes and wide roads. Industries are grouped together in one area. There is evidence of central planning.

Old European Cities

There are dense streets in the center of town. Some geometric pattern, especially converging roads, can be seen. Canals are often in evidence. Airports are in the outer part of the city and the suburbs are likely to be cross-hatched.

Geology

Analyzing geological formations is very complex and requires a geologist skilled in remote sensing. Usually the infrared and thermal infrared bands are the most useful to this type of analysis. However, geologists often study drainage in order to understand the local geology.

Sloping Formations
Drainage patterns and creeks usually run in a parallel pattern. Usually the steeper the formation, the more parallel the drainage.

Flat Geology
The drainage pattern wanders and slowly gathers into larger rivers. From a satellite, the pattern looks like the branches of a tree.

Limestone
Drainage is less common and sinkholes with water are often found as water runs underground.

Faults
Drainage patterns suddenly change course as they run along the faults.

Hills
Drainage is usually radial as the water runs off each side.

Industry

Both military intelligence and urban studies need to find and identify industries. Usually a true-color composite is the best.

Blue is easily scattered by pollutants, so it can identify smoke plumes, and red is a good band for manmade objects. Mid or thermal infrared can also help identify heat sources.

The first goal in interpretation is to classify the industry as mining, fabrication, energy dependent processes, or chemical dependent processes. Obviously, the larger the facility, the easier it is to identify.

Mining

Open pits are the most obvious, because they scar acres of land. Generally, open pit operations mine low value, high volume ores that lie near the surface. Some materials mined in open pits are copper, gold, gravel, sand, iron, bauxite, coal, peat, etc. One clue to the type of material mined is whether it's processed at the site. Iron ore and bauxite are usually processed elsewhere because they need large quantities of energy. Generally, there are large roads or transportation facilities in order to move the ore.

Low grade ores like gold and copper can be processed at the site with heap leaching. Evidence of heap leaching is three or four ponds used for holding the solution near the processing area. Higher grade ores are often shipped elsewhere, although smelters can be found at the site.

Gravel and sand are usually processed at the site and the pits often contain water.

Underground mines are for valuable, deep, large mineral deposits. They are harder to locate, but they are found near mineralized zones and usually have roads or tracks leading into a side of a mountain or disappearing underground.

Energy Dependent Processes

Producing steel, aluminum, or other metals often requires large amounts of energy. These sites can often be recognized because they have coal piles, electricity, right-of-ways, or dams nearby. They are often near major rail lines because they process large quantities of raw materials. Mid or thermal infrared bands show large amounts of heat.

Chemical Dependent Processes

Petroleum, nitric and sulfuric acid, plastics, and explosives are processed in this manner. The site is usually recognized by virtue of tanks and pipelines. In the case of petroleum processing, there are few loading docks because the materials are moved through pipelines.

Fabrication

Manufacturing is harder to recognize because of the many different sizes the product can take. The size of the final product and production levels can be determined by the size of transportation facilities at the facility.

Naval And Maritime Facilities

Analysts want to be able to tell the difference between military and civilian facilities. Usually true color images are best because blue, green, and red light can help show water depth. If you need to define the shoreline, use infrared because it's absorbed by the water.

Naval Base

Naval facilities usually have many small piers and isolated bunkers for ammunition. There is also an airfield and sometimes a cement apron, extending into the water, for seaplanes.

Civilian Facility

Maritime facilities usually have large, long piers with warehouses nearby (often on the piers). Since they are usually shipping to points inland, there are rail facilities and loading docks. Facilities are often crowded, so it isn't unusual to find ships anchored in the bay.

Drydocks and Repair Facilities

Drydocks are usually rectangular notches in the shoreline. There are usually large buildings nearby.

Water

Slow moving water is often green from algae. If the water is clear, underwater objects that only reflect blue are between 90 to 150 feet deep. If it reflects blue and green, it's between 30 and 90 feet deep. If it reflects blue, green and red, it is less than 30 feet deep. Since the water is often murky, judging depth with the blue and green bands is risky.

If the water is too clear, the analyst may not be able to tell if the object is above or under the water. In that case, use an infrared band. Since water absorbs infrared, underwater objects will disappear while those above water will still be visible.

Soil

Identifying the different types of soil and the water content is useful for farming and civil engineering. It's also important to military planners who want to find routes that can hold vehicles. Since moisture is noticeable in the mid-infrared group, usually LANDSAT bands 5 and 7 are used.

Transportation

The sophistication of the transportation network is an indication of the level of civilization. Modern, First World countries have extensive networks, while the rest of the world usually has limited transportation. Since the analyst is looking for manmade objects, the true-color composite is usually the best.

Railroads

These are gently sweeping lines on the image. Short parallel lines are sidings, and lines usually converge in the center of a city for the terminal. Railroads are more likely to be found near industrial facilities.

Canals

They are dark lines with heavier vegetation along the sides. Since canals were usually built over a hundred years ago, they indicate older societies.

Local Roads

These are slower roads, so they tend to meander more and have more angles.

Expressways

These have gently sweeping lines like railroads, but they have cloverleafs and merging lanes for traffic.

Vegetation

Satellite imagery is excellent for tracking the progress of crops. The best color composite is the color infrared image, with red light represented by blue, mid-infrared light represented by green, and near-infrared light represented by red.

Fallow Land

Usually this is grey or white.

Planted Land

This starts as a light green, but becomes darker as the crop matures.

Plant Health

Healthy plants are a bright green, while unhealthy plants are a dark green color. Coniferous forests (pines) are poor reflectors of infrared, so don't mistake them for ill vegetation.

Farm Size

Farms in communist societies are usually larger than their counterparts in the capitalistic world. Private farmers own smaller plots and usually split them among several crops in order to diversify risk.

Summary

Satellite data is worthless unless you know how to present and analyze it. Although there are several different products available and the combinations appear to be limitless, there are a few methods that allow the analyst to gain the maximum amount of information for the minimum effort. Except for true color and color infrared, the best solution is to select one band of light from each of the three major light groups. This allows you to avoid duplication and provides you with the largest amount of information in each image.

Obviously, what I've covered here is only a small part of image interpretation. It does, however, give you an idea of what analysts look for in their work. If you need to know more about the art of interpretation, please read the books listed in the Bibliography.

14

Sources For Satellite Imagery and Related Material

Satellite Companies

SPOT Image Corporation
Sells imagery from the French SPOT satellite.
(703) 620-2200
1897 Preston White Dr.
Reston, VA 22091-4368

EOSAT
Sells imagery from LANDSAT.
(800) 344-9933
4300 Forbes Blvd.
Lanham, MD 20706

Central Trading Systems
The US representative for Soviet satellite imagery.
(817) 731-9102
5724 Cedar Creek Rd.
Fort Worth, TX 76109

Jet Propulsion Laboratories
JPL holds the US radar imagery.
Currently there isn't any way to order the information.
4800 Oak Grove Dr.
Pasadena, CA 91109

EROS
They sell aerial photographs, some radar images, and photo-graphs from US manned space missions.
(605) 594-6151
Geological Survey Customer Service
EROS Data Center
Sioux Falls, SD 57198

Defense Mapping Agency
Military units that need satellite imagery should contact them.
Write to:
Director
DMA Hydrographic/Topographic Center
ATTN: SDTFl
6500 Brookes Lane
Washington, D.C. 20315-0030

Value Added Services

Barranger Laboratories
They specialize in interpreting satellite imagery.
(303) 277-1687
15000 W 6th Avenue Suite 300
Golden, CO 80401

The Orthoshop
They make maps and correct satellite imagery.
(602) 798-1323
1121 W Grant Rd., Ste 401
Tucson, AZ 85705

Reference Materials

Autometric Inc.
They produce the excellent *Multispectral Users Guide*. They also
provide other satellite interpretation services.
(703) 658-4000
5301 Shawnee Rd.
Alexandria, VA 22312-2312

American Society for Photogrammetry and Remote Sensing
The professional society for people involved in satellite imagery.
(301) 493-0290
5410 Grosvenor Lane, Ste 210
Bethesda, MD 20814-2160

Part IV

Future Applications
and
Implications

15

Trends in
Satellite Technology
and Uses

Satellite imagery is thirty years old and commercial applications were just recognized twenty years ago. There is no doubt, especially considering the growing number of commercial satellites in space, that more will be learned as the systems improve.

Technology

Many of these advances will be made thanks to the electronic revolution that started in the Seventies. The advances that brought forth the CCD was just the beginning. The future will see smaller and more sensitive sensors. That will improve commercial resolution, and when the atmosphere prevents any more improvements, will allow higher altitudes, which will give satellites longer lives.

As sensors become more sensitive, we can expect to see new bands open up. Until now, we were limited to looking at light the atmosphere transmitted. As sensors improve, we can look at light absorbed by the atmosphere. This will give us a better chance to study the atmosphere, especially effects of pollution, and open up new views of the earth.

The declining price of computing power and memory will have a direct impact on the use of remote sensing. Sensors can be tied into computers in order to sort through data and cheaper computers will allow more people and companies to use digital imagery. In fact, if present trends hold true, computers that can manipulate satellite imagery will find themselves in homes before the end of the century.

More powerful computers will inevitably lead to more break-throughs in enhancement and interpretation. Analysts aren't in danger of losing their jobs, but many of the mundane tasks will be done by computers and preliminary interpretation software will become available to the public.

The day when the earth will be under constant coverage is also approaching. The US intelligence community can cover hot spots several times a day, but improved sensors will inevitably allow satellites to sit in a geosynchronous orbit and constantly monitor parts of the globe. The advantages for the intelligence community are obvious, but they can also help monitor natural disasters and other fast-moving events.

Constant coverage isn't important without real-time viewing. The current generation of US spy satellites offers virtual real-time viewing in some cases. But the real benefit will be when the field commander can see enemy deployments as the battle rages. The fog of war will finally lift a little.

It's impossible to foresee all the changes in satellite imagery. Prior to the 1960s, many experts thought satellite photographs were impractical because they were too far away. They were wrong. What "impossibilities" will be proven false in the future, I can't foretell. However, the future is bright.

Satellites and Secrecy

The future is definitely bright for satellite imagery, but much of its future is in the hands of the government. Can the government help or hinder its growth?

While the secret technology of the stealth bomber is available at most bookstores, the history, technology, and products of America's reconnaissance satellites are still shrouded in secrecy. Today you have a better chance of looking at the stealth fighter than the first satellite photos brought back by Discoverer XIV over 30 years ago. The reasons behind this decision give us an insight into the minds of the intelligence community, their attitudes towards democracy, and possibly a chilling vision of the future.

The intelligence community's refusal to allow the dissemination of any information is an excellent example of the bureaucratic thinking within the Capital beltway. Reconnaissance satellites are a well-known fact and have been widely reported by the press. The Soviets know about the satellites and their capabilities, especially since William Kampiles sold them the manual to the KH-11. US arms negotiators have shown satellite photos to their counterparts from the USSR. Even the 30-year-old photos of the Soviet Union are crude compared to the commercial photos available from LANDSAT, SPOT, or even the Soviets. Yet the intelligence community has fought like a tiger to keep even the first photo from being released.

Every administration since Johnson's has had strong reasons to release satellite photos. LBJ and Reagan wanted to use photos to show the Soviet threat. Nixon and Carter needed to show satellite photos to convince a wary Congress and public that SALT agreements could be verified. Despite the pressure from these democratically elected leaders, the people in the National

Reconnaissance Office have resisted, while creating additional bureaucratic obstacles.

In 1978, in the midst of the SALT II Treaty negotiations, President Carter wanted to lift the veil on spy satellites in order to reassure the public that the US could prevent Soviet cheating. Declassification was favored by Carter, the Secretary of State, the Arms Control Director, and even the Director of the CIA and other intelligence types. The opposition came from some in the military intelligence community, who promised to declassify some photos after developing procedures to handle it (over 10 years later, the procedures haven't been developed as promised). But the major blow came from Department of Defense lawyers who argued that a declassification might lead to a flood of freedom of information requests for other information (even though that didn't happen with U-2 and SR-71 photos). Secrecy had won out over democracy once again.

Despite the wishes of our elected leaders and the arguments of some in the intelligence community, secrecy still shrouds the spy satellite program. Why? The answer comes from the fears of bureaucrats and government officials who don't have to answer to the voters.

One of the first rules of government workers is, "Knowledge is power." Since satellite information is now used by many other parts of the government, such as law enforcement, by controlling the source of information, the intelligence community now has some control over the actions of other agencies, such as the Drug Enforcement Agency, the FBI, and Customs. The intelligence community now knows it can count on support from these agencies in Congressional debates.

Declassifying information will expose mistakes made years ago. Rather than risk embarrassment, the intelligence community would condemn the information to top secret dustbins.

Finally, release of information about spy satellites would reveal that they have been used against US citizens. While most of the public supports their use against the enemies of the US, most voters would probably change their attitudes towards reconnaissance satellites if they knew how extensive the spying has been. It's better, the bureaucrats reason, that this explosive issue never surfaces.

As this book has explained, satellite imagery is a powerful tool for making our world better. We can manage our environment and resources much better than we could have ever imagined. Yet, the technology for making these tools better is denied to the citizen while it is used by the government without check. History has shown us that a government that doesn't have any limits on its actions uses its power for repression. History also shows us that a tool reserved for governments becomes a tool for tyranny. If the heavens are restricted to the citizen and the halls of government are left without supervision, maybe we will become the servants while the satellites remain the spies.

Satellites and Civil Liberties

"The right of the people to be secure in their persons, houses, papers, and effects, against unreasonable searches and seizures shall not be violated."
— Fourth Amendment, US Constitution

In the 1980s, the Supreme Court made several rulings that established the legal basis for satellite surveillance. Some of these key rulings are:

California vs. Ciraolo, 1986. The Court said aerial photography didn't interfere with a person's expectation of privacy or society's recognition of privacy. 106 S.Ct. 1809, 1810 (1986).

United States vs. Dunn, 1987. The Court held that open areas aren't covered by the Fourth Amendment protection. 55 U.S.L.W. 4251, 4253.

Dow Chemical Company vs. The United States, 1986. This set forth standards regarding when aerial photography is legal. It did express concern about satellite surveillance, but didn't establish any legal distinction between the two. 106 S.Ct. 1819 (1986).

The Dow case is the most far reaching of these rulings because it set forth the legal rationale for overhead imagery. Although they didn't specifically include satellites, the rationale for their ruling against Dow set the stage for the legal use of satellites.

Dow had been found guilty of pollution violations on the basis of aerial photography. They appealed on the basis that overflying the facility had violated the Fourth Amendment, because it was a violation of privacy and there hadn't been any warrant as prescribed in the Constitution.

The justices ruled against Dow in a 5 to 4 decision that set four standards for judging the legality of aerial photography. They are:

Open Fields Doctrine

The justices ruled that the Dow factory was like an open field and therefore subject to observation. This was especially true since aircraft overflights are so common that to assume you won't be observed from overhead is unreasonable. They also noted that Dow hadn't made any provision to protect itself from overhead photography; therefore, they couldn't expect any privacy.

Invasiveness of the Sensor

The majority opinion noted that the aerial sensors couldn't penetrate the walls of the factory to record hidden information, therefore, it didn't fall under the protection accorded to the individual against electronic eavesdropping.

This could become an important issue because thermal-infrared and mid-infrared sensors can detect heat from objects indoors. Defense lawyers could argue that such sensors fall into the same category as electronic eavesdropping equipment. However, it is likely, considering the "law and order" attitude of today's Supreme Court, that they will rule that temperature differences noticeable from the outside are legal evidence. This will probably be ruled on soon as temperature sensing becomes more important in finding underground marijuana crops.

Availability of the Equipment

The court noted that general sensing equipment is legal for surveillance because it's commonly available. In this regard, they noted that satellites were suspect because the images were not available to the public. However, thanks to commercial satellite imagery, this distinction disappears. Of course, one could still argue against evidence brought by military satellites because that quality of equipment isn't available to the public.

Intention to Uncover Secrets

The court noted that the purpose of satellite imagery isn't to uncover secrets and has many legitimate purposes in geography and mapping. Therefore, any accidental discovery of illegal activity is legitimate.

The rationale set forth by the Supreme Court establishes the foundation for satellite surveillance. However, there are other factors that have an impact on the use of satellites in intruding on privacy.

Warrants

The Constitution only protects against unreasonable searches without a warrant. Once a warrant is issued, there is nothing that stops the government from using any satellite intelligence it can obtain. Of course, a warrant can only be issued with probable cause, but that isn't a major barrier for the police.

A warrant isn't needed if the overhead surveillance is part of a plan. For instance, the EPA can conduct overhead surveillance as part of determining air quality and any pollution detected is admissible as evidence.

Altitude

Once aerial photography was made legal, police units started buzzing suspected criminals at dangerously low heights. One police helicopter sat a few feet over a house while a drug agent looked through a skylight to see if a plant was in fact marijuana. Although it hasn't gone to the Supreme Court, several state courts have ruled that altitude does affect the invasiveness of the surveillance.

Military Assistance

The 1982 Posse Comitatus Law allows the military to help the police even though it can't enforce the law. As a result, it's legal for the Keyhole satellites to become part of the law enforcement effort. This is especially evident in the drug war.

Poisoned Fruit

The exclusionary rule held evidence obtained in an unconstitutional way couldn't be used as evidence. Originally this also meant that any evidence gathered as a result of learning something from an unconstitutional act was also excluded. However, the Court has ruled such evidence is admissible if it could have been obtained in a legal manner. In other words, even if unconstitutional satellite imagery leads law enforcement towards clues that convict the defendant, that evidence can be held admissible if it would have been found another way (say, with aerial photography).

Uses Outside the Law

The use of satellite imagery doesn't even fall under the protection granted by the Constitution if they show locations outside the country. Therefore, military imagery can be used to find and attack drug installations in South America or Asia. Nor does the Constitution count if the evidence is not brought to court. For instance, satellite imagery can be used if the police want to trace someone and have no intention of using the evidence in court. This is technically illegal, but no one would know about it.

Protecting Your Privacy

One issue mentioned in the Dow case was that in order to expect privacy and protect yourself from warrantless searches, precautions should be taken against aerial surveillance. Therefore, someone protecting their property from satellites (see Chapter 11) can expect more privacy and may have a better legal defense against satellite imagery than the person who does nothing.

Public Good

In many cases the courts have ruled that some violations of constitutional rights are to be expected in the public good. That means if they want you, they can get you.

As the Dow case showed us, it's legal to use satellite imagery. As resolution becomes finer and the military satellites are used by more law enforcement agencies, government surveillance will grow. Unless the Supreme Court sets firm standards on overhead surveillance, this country has taken one more step on the path that will lead to a society like that in *1984.*

Future Directions

Big Brother aside, there is great potential for satellite imagery. There are several fields that will probably experience growth during the future. Some of them are:

Media
Satellite images are now a part of the news when they want to cover wars. As they become more familiar with the technology and resolution becomes finer, there will be more applications. Newsmen will use images of cities to show locations of stories and even give the public an idea of the size of some events. Imagine the day when a Monday Night Football game has satellite coverage instead of a blimp (don't laugh, the Keyhole satellites can see as much as the camera on the Goodyear blimp).

Geological Applications
Although geology was one of the first civilian applications, there is still much to learn. New methods are helping geologists find mineral deposits faster and with more certainty than before. Since millions are spent each year in exploration, there will be more money available for research into satellite image applications.

Mapping
Our world is moving faster and becoming more accurate. We can't afford to spend years making maps that are obsolete when they are published. Satellites offer a solution. With them, mapping agencies can make new maps in weeks instead of years.

Environmental
This field offers the most growth potential. Not only can governments use it for enforcement, companies can use it to

monitor their own emissions. One of the biggest advantages, however, is that scientists can measure the true effects of pollution on the earth.

Artistic

Many people like the beauty of satellite images. As the imagery becomes more common and resolution becomes finer, expect to see poster/maps that show localities or popular sites. Who knows, maybe one of these days the college bookstore will sell satellite image posters of the campus.

Engineering

Aerial photography is important to engineers. The only reason satellites haven't been as popular is that the resolution is limited. When commercial satellites have the resolution of the Keyhole satellites, we can expect to see more civil engineering applications.

Perspective

My first serious encounter with satellite imagery was the *National Geographic* mosaic of the United States in the July, 1976 issue. I spread it out on the table and looked at familiar sights. I could see familiar rivers and with their help locate many cities. Suddenly I realized that the US wasn't as large as I thought.

The thought was driven home a few months ago when I saw one LANDSAT image of the Middle East that included Syria, Lebanon, Israel, and Jordan. The resolution was so good I could see runways, highways, and even airplanes. Yet as small as this area is (a healthy Boy Scout can walk between the capitals of the four countries), there were immense walls between the people. Maybe if they looked at a photograph like that, they would realize they were close neighbors.

16

Conclusion

Does satellite imagery promise a better new world or a "Brave New World?" Currently, most satellite imagery is used by the government as it searches for weapons, enemies, and criminals. If the Supreme Court encourages this use, we're headed towards a perverted new Dark Ages.

There is something we can do to stop this trend — use satellites for private and commercial uses. Commercial use will encourage launching more private satellites that aren't controlled by the government. It will help us wrest a bit of control from those in power.

Increased use of satellite imagery will also alert the public to the risks. If the American people realize the power of overhead surveillance, they can act to protect themselves through laws or other restrictions.

Demand for more satellite imagery will also convince the government to let scientists use advanced sensors for commercial imagery. Better sensors will lead to more discoveries and lower costs.

Finally, commercial imagery can act as a check on the powers of government. With it, the media corrected the State Department when it misread a fire at the Libyan chemical plant. They can also use it to monitor government actions that aren't in the best interest of the people.

Remember, technology isn't evil, just the people who employ it. Technology is only a tool, its effects depend upon how it is used.

The freedom to use satellite imagery is here and the opportunity to keep it a tool of the people is available. Use it!

Appendix
Satellite Systems
Currently in Use

ALMAZ
Country: USSR
Spacecraft: Cosmos
Start of program: 1987
Program completion:
 Not known
Resolution: 30 feet
Optical system type: Radar
Data return: Digital

KFA-1000, MK-4
Country: USSR
Spacecraft: Cosmos,
 Resource-FI
Start of program: 1975
Program completion:
 Not known
Resolution: 15 feet

Optical system type:
 Photographic
Data return: Capsules

KH-4A, CORONA
Country: USA
Spacecraft: Thor-Agena D
Start of program: 1963
Program completion: 1967
Resolution: 10 feet
Optical system type:
 Photographic
Data return: 2 capsules
Number of successful
 launches: 47

KH-4B, CORONA
Country: USA
Spacecraft: Thor-Agena D

Start of program: 1966
Program completion: 1972
Resolution: 5 feet

Optical system type:
  Photographic
Data Return: 2 capsules
Number of successful
  launches: 33

KH-7, GAMBIT
Country: USA
Spacecraft: Atlas-Agena D
Start of program: 1963
Program completion: 1967
Resolution: 18 inches
Optical system type:
  Photographic
Data return: 2 capsules
Number of successful
  launches: 36

KH-8, GAMBIT
Country: USA
Spacecraft: Titan 3B-
  Agena D
Start of program: 1966
Program completion: 1984
Resolution: 6 inches
Optical system type:
  Photographic
Data return: 2 capsules
Number of successful
  launches: 50

KH-9, HEXAGON
Country: USA
Spacecraft: Titan
Start of program: 1971
Program completion: 1986
Resolution: 2 feet
Optical system type:
  Photographic
Data return: 4 capsules
Number of successful
  launches: 19

KH-11, KENNAN, CRYSTAL
Country: USA
Spacecraft: Titan or Shuttle
Start of program: 1976
Program completion: Still
  operating
Resolution: 3-6 inches
Optical system type: Electric
  (CCD)
Data return: Digital
Number of successful
  launches: 8 plus

LANDSAT
Country: USA
Spacecraft: Thor and Titan
Start of program: 1972
Program completion: Still
  operating
Resolution: 90 feet
Optical system type: Electric

(Vidicon at first, now
CCD)
Data return: Digital
Number of successful
   launches: 5 plus

SPOT
Country: France
Spacecraft: Ariane
Start of program: 1986
Program completion: Still
   operating
Resolution: 30 feet
Optical system type: Electric
   (CCD)
Data return: Digital
Number of successful
   launches: 2 plus

Bibliography

Adam, John. "Peacekeeping by Technical Means." *IEEE Spectrum*. July, 1986. p. 2.

Avery, T. Eugene, *Interpretation of Aerial Photography*. Burgess Publishing Company, Minneapolis, MN, 1968.

Ford, Cimino, and Elachi. *Space Shuttle Columbia Views the World With Imaging Radar: The SIR-A Experiment*. Jet Propulsion Laboratory, Pasadena, CA, 1982.

Ford, Cimino, Holt, and Ruzek. *Shuttle Imaging Radar Views the Earth from Challenger: The SIR-B Experiment*. Jet Propulsion Laboratory, Pasadena, CA, 1986.

Hough, Harold. *A Practical Guide to Photographic Intelligence*. Loompanics Unlimited, Port Townsend, WA, 1990.

Kienko, Yu. "Remote Sensing of the Earth from Space for Studying and Mapping Natural and Economic Potentialities in the USSR."

Lillesand, Thomas and Kiefer, Ralph. *Remote Sensing and Image Interpretation.*, John Wiley & Sons, New York, 1979.

Richelson, Jeffrey. *America's Secret Eyes in Space.* Harper & Row, New York, 1990.

Talbett, Micheal. "Satellite Surveillance and the Fourth Amendment." *Pecora XI Symposium Proceedings.* pg. 209.

Wolf, Paul. *Elements of Photogrammetry.* McGraw-Hill Book Company, New York, 1973.

Multispectral Users Guide. Autometric Inc., Alexandria, VA, 1990.

LANDSAT Information. EOSAT. Landham, MD, 1990.

SPOT Information. SPOT Image Corp. Reston, VA. 1990.

Soviet Satellite Information. Central Trading Systems. Fort Worth, TX. 1990.

Glossary

Band A segment of the electromagnetic spectrum.

CCD Charged Coupled Device A solid state sensor that detects visible and some infrared light. This device offers real-time viewing and fine resolution. Can be as small as one micron.

Contrast The range of tones in an image. A high contrast image ranges from pure white to black. A low contrast image uses only a small range of greys.

Discoverer The first US spy satellite system.

Enhancement Methods for improving the satellite image.

Geographic Information Systems (GIS) A database that provides information based on location. Often used for mapping.

Keyhole The US military reconnaissance satellite system.

LANDSAT The US commercial satellite system.

Middle Infrared 1.5 to 2.35 microns. It can detect moisture content.

Multispectral   Capable of detecting many different bands of light.

Near Infrared   .75 to .9 microns. Best for detecting vegetation.

Orthophotography   A method for correcting photographs. Often used in mapping.

Panchromatic   A black and white image that covers many different bands of light.

Photogrammetry   The science of measuring objects based on photographs.

Pixel   Means picture element. This is the smallest unit of information in a television image. The equivalent of one dot on our television screen.

Principal Component Analysis   An enhancement method that better separates information.

Ratio Image   An enhancement method that compares the reflection from different bands of light.

Remote Sensing   Measuring data from a remote location just by observing the object.

Resolution   The smallest object that can be detected by a satellite.

Spacial   The characteristics of an image that relate to shapes.

Spectral   The characteristics of an image that refer to the type of light reflected.

SPOT   The French satellite system.

Thermal Infrared   Energy emitted by objects because of their temperature. 10.5 to 12.5 microns.

Visible Band   .4 to .7 microns. This represents the blue, green, and red light.

Index

YOU WILL ALSO WANT TO READ: